LIFE OF A HUSTLER
IN CHICAGO

All inquiries should be addressed to:

Book Domain LLC.
543 E Louise Dr Phoenix, Az 85050

Ordering Information:
Amount Deals. Special rebates are accessible on the amount bought by corporations, associations, and others. For points of interest, contact the distributor at the address above.

Printed in the United States of America.

ISBN-13   Paperback: 978-1-967903-10-8
                eBook: 978-1-967903-09-2

LIFE OF A HUSTLER
IN CHICAGO

AL WYNN ROSS

BOOK DOMAIN LLC
Publish to Perfection

CHAPTER 1

The paddy wagon backed up through the big iron gates into the jail yard and about 35 inmates stepped out of the truck. Three guards came from the jailhouse to help the other guards take in the new prisoners. We lined up in a single file as they took the handcuffs off. We were led into the dining room to a tin pan of greasy salt pork and beans, but being in court all day made those beans taste like steak. When we finished eating, we were led to a shower room where we were led into a shower room. They sprayed us for lice or any other bugs. After that, we were issued clothing and a couple of blankets and sheets.

After we sat around for hours on benches, we were assigned to our cell. I was assigned to lock up G-3. It was getting late when we reached the cells it was almost time for lockdown. You could hear the big doors slamming back as the inmates marched into their cells. I was in cell #17 on the top bunk. Another elderly guy had the bottom bunk, and as I passed him, he said, "My name is Fisher, young blood." I said, "My name is Al Wynn."

He said, "Where are you from?' As the big iron door slammed behind us. I answered "47th Street." He said, "Oh, you live on the south side, I live on the west side, on Jackson." I replied, "I used to live on Jackson years ago." "I can't say what black it was because it was so long ago," I told him as I climbed onto my bunk. I was exhausted. So, I didn't fix the bunk with the sheets. I crawled onto my bunk with my clothes on and put the blanket over me. I thought I would take care of all that the next day, as I heard the old man say good night, and I closed my eyes and went to sleep.

The next morning at about 6:00, the doors opened with a bang. You could hear the guards saying, "OK, on the chow!" The inmates started running past each other, and some of them were running to take showers while others were washing up in the bowl. Most of the inmates who didn't wash up or take a shower went straight to the table and sat down. Mr. Fisher and I sat at the far-end table to the right. Two tables were lined up on the east and west sides of the room, with 30 inmates in a cell house and fifteen at two tables.

After everyone was seated for about fifteen minutes, the tin pans and cups came up on a dumb waiter. The inmate who ran the floor was called the barn boss. He issued the food out. He made sure that the day room, as they call it, was clean, and he had five or six helpers. They ran it like they were the police and all five or six of them would whip your ass like they were the goon squad, and the guards would ignore the whole episode like nothing was happening. The barn boss ran the show inside of that cell house. The barn boss ran the gambling, and he ran the store and the loan sharking. The three things were run just like they ran them in the streets, only cigarettes were the money.

After we ate, the barn boss and his henchmen would wash the dishes, and the inmates would put the chairs on the tables, and then they would have to go back to their cells to wait for the count as the day room was swept and mopped. After about 45 minutes, we were let out to the dayroom, and all the cells were locked. There was only one way for us to go back into the cell, which would have been if they had a recount or if that person had a visitor. Other than that, we would have a full day in the dayroom. We had a television set in front of us, and it was nearly 10' above our heads, but most of the time the guys would be playing cards, dominoes, or gambling with dice and poker. It was business as usual every day in the dayroom.

We spent all evening in the dayroom. Mr. Fisher and I were sitting near the guard in front of the room when I saw him for the first time. He had come out of the hallway from the cell room dressed in his drawers and nice-looking house shoes with a towel thrown across his shoulder. I looked up at the clock and it said 8:30 AM. I looked at Mr. Fisher. said, "What is this man?" "Who in the hell is he?" He said, "Who?" I said, "That white guy over there." "Who is he, a damn guard?" He said, "No, man, he is the head of the Mafia." I said, "Man, stop bullshitting." He said, "Man, I'm not playing, he's been here for a year and he's under investigation." "You haven't read about him in the papers?" I said, "No!" He said, "Yeah, man, he gets up about the same time every day, and he doesn't eat with us, either." "You'll see him about 9:00 AM getting the hell out of here." "He must be with the warden or something." "We don't know where he goes or when he leaves here, but he'll be back about 6:00 for the count."

Mr. Fisher and I were playing tonk when I saw him again coming out of the cell block. He was dressed now in a blue silk jumpsuit with short sleeves. It was the kind of jumpsuit that had a side pull elastic belt with a gold hook in the front. He walked straight ahead to the cell door by the guard. He looked at the black guard and said, "OK, Jimmy, I'm ready." The guard opened the door. The iron gate door closed behind him, and they walked about three or four feet to a solid door. The blackguard, Jimmy, took his key and opened the steel door, and Frank Caleni vanished through the opening.

The next day or two, I lay around resting and looking at the television and the game with Mr. Fisher while learning what most of the players called themselves and the inner crowd of people's names that hung around with the mafia, the barn boss, and his cronies. I let Mr. Fisher peek at my commissary slip; in other words, I let him see how much money I had in the books, and it was $350.00. That was the money the institution kept for me, and I could spend it in the grocery store. So, he gladly let me have a pack of cigarettes or whatever else that I needed.

Now, on the third day, I went to Mr. Fisher, and I said, "Hey man, I want to get in that dice game." "Who do I go to for the cigarettes that I need until I go to the store?" He said, "Of course, you go to Leroy, the barn boss." "How many cigarettes do you need?" I said, "To start with, three cartons." He said, "He's going to charge you five packs on each carton of cigarettes that you get, so if you want three cartons, it's going to cost you a carton and a half of the three cartons." I asked him, "Well, how do I go about getting these cigarettes?" He said, "Well, I'll introduce you to Leroy, and all you have to do is show him how much money you have on the books."

We approached Leroy for the cigarettes. He was a big, dark guy who needed a shave, and he seemed like he needed his hair combed because it was long and nappy. He wore his jeans and shirt loose. His arms were big as though he used to be a weightlifter, but now there was just fat there. He looked at me and said, "You know that these three cartons will cost you a carton and a half??" I said, "Yes." He asked me, "Do you have the money on the books?" I replied, "Yes," and showed him the slip. He asked me, "Are you going back to trial, or did you get your time already?" I replied, "I got my time already." He asked, "How much time did you get?" I answered, "A year in Sandstone." He asked, "When are you going to be shipped out?" I told him, "I don't know, they haven't told me yet." He went on saying, "Well, I can't give you the cigarettes today because we have to check out your ship-out date." "I can't give you the cigarettes today and they ship you out tomorrow, store day isn't until Wednesday." "You have to give me a day for the cigarettes." I said, "OK, I'll wait until tomorrow."

That evening I saw him talking to Frank Caleni. Then in another half an hour or so, Calaeni was talking to Jimmy, the guard. Before lockdown, I had forgotten about cigarettes, the barn boss, or Caleni. I was interested in a domino game that was getting heated up at one of the tables. Someone tapped me on my back softly. I turned and faced the barn boss, Leroy. He said, "You'll be shipped out on Friday after next." "You can get the cigarettes." "It's not going to do you much good now they're fixing to lock us down." He said, "You can get the cigarettes first thing in the morning, and I'll give you a list of the things that I want in return." I said, "Bet!"

CHAPTER 2

Early the next morning, after the count and we were let out of our cells, one of Leroy's henchmen came to me with three cartons of cigarettes. He gave me the cigarettes as I stepped into the dayroom. He said, "Leroy told me to give you these." I said, "Thanks." I continued to the washroom. I noticed Leroy standing in the middle of the floor, staring at me. I bowed my head to him. He bowed his head back. I continued into the bathroom with the henchman following me. He went on talking, "So, what kind of gambling do you do, dominoes, pity pat, tonk, what do you like to play?" I said, "I just like dice, man." "I can play it all, but I like dice." He said, "Good, that's what I like." "Leroy starts his dice game at about 10:00." "You're welcome to come over if you'd like." I said, "Good." He turned and walked away. I, in turn, walked into the stall.

It was about 9:30 and Mr. Fisher and I were playing tonk. Mr. Fisher didn't gamble, so we played for fun. He said, "What kind of gambling are you going to do?" I said, "Dice. He said, "Well, you be careful over there because some of those guys are kind of slick." "They know that Leroy has peeped at your whole card." "They know how much money you've got on the books, and everybody is going to try to get it before you get shipped out of here."

It was about fifteen minutes after 10:00 when I went over to the dice blanket that was between the first table and the kitchen. About six guys were standing around the blanket and Leroy and his henchmen were on their knees with their feet to the wall. I watched the game there for about ten minutes and right away I could tell what was going down. Leroy cupped the 3rd dice under his thumb, and his henchman Joe had the miss outs and they were working their little circle well. So, I eased into the game with three packs of cigarettes. Joe faded me. I caught a ten, and after three rolls, I threw a seven. The dice were passed to the next guy. That guy shot two packs of cigarettes. I faded him. The guy caught a six. "Three packs, you don't six," I said to the shooter. He said, "Bet!"

He came out with the dice, and they read seven. I collected on the bet. The dice went to the next shooter. The dice game went that way up and down until late into the evening when the dice got to Leroy and Joe. I thought to myself, I would shoot one pack, but no more than two. I made most of my money from side bets. That evening I won twelve packs of cigarettes, making me have a total of four cartons and two packs.

The next day I made about five packs. I wasn't trying to show my skills because Joe kept throwing me the missouts. I knew I would lose to them, so I stuck to side bets. After the fifth day, my luck improved. Joe was sent to Joliet. His other henchmen didn't know the switch like Joe did. So, that left Leroy at a disadvantage; he could only make the switch with the third dice. The load was too heavy for him to do both, and I peeped at it. He had to use the straight dice throughout most of the game. Leroy was shocked that Sunday evening when the dice came to me. It seemed like half of the cell house was watching the game, including the Mafia. "Five packs I shoot," I said. It was Leroy's turn to fade me. He said, "Shoot em, I've got you covered."

Without hesitation, I picked up the one and locked the one into the five. I shook them up to my ear and let them spin with the navy spin. The dice came out at eleven. I said, "OK, guys, I'm shooting all of it." One guy said, "How much you got, Leroy?" Leroy said, "I've got three." One guy said, "I've got three." Another guy said, "I've got the four." I grabbed the dice and locked them into "the seven." Instead of coming with the navy spin, I let them march down that blanket like soldiers. The dice stopped on a 4 and a five, nine. I shot for that nine three times before it came six, tray, nine.

There were two cartons up there on the floor. I looked at Leroy. He looked at me with a weird stare. I said, "Well, fellows, I'm going to take this down." "Shoot two packs!" The guy next to me said, "I've got the two, unless you want it, Leroy." Leroy said, "No, you can have it." I locked them on 12 and the dice came out one, two, crap. The dice were passed on. The guy shot three packs, and I shot the other three. I faded him. He caught a ten. Two or three rows he seven out. I was back even with the board. I kind of slacked up on my shooting the dice as I noticed Leroy and the Mafia staring at me.

The dice game almost ended because only Leroy and I had the winnings. About half an hour later, everyone's eyes were on the television listening to the news. I was surprised to see Caleni standing in front of me. He said, "I noticed you play tonk, Al." I said, "Yes." He said, "What about a couple of games for fun?" I said, "Ok, deal them." I don't know if he let me win or not, but for the games in a row, I won. I smiled at him. I said, "Loser's deal, man, it's yours." "Deal." He smiled. He said, "What do you do in the street, Al? Do you gamble?" I said, "Not with cards, I shoot a little dice." He said, "Yeah, I see." "You're very lucky." We played about five more games; I told him that I was a contractor by trade. He just looked at me and kind of smiled. He never told me what he did, and I didn't ask him.

CHAPTER 3

It was on a Wednesday, two days before being shipped out to Sandstone. I had eight cartons of cigarettes, and I could only take one to Sandstone. So, I made a deal with Leroy by giving him two cartons to let Mr. Fisher run his store with five cartons. Mr. Fisher was doing a year. He had about seven months left to do, and if he ran the store right, those five cartons would help him through. He had children on the outside and a drunken wife. He would hear from his wife now and then, but never anything from his children. He thanked me a thousand times for those cigarettes. He asked me if I was ever on the west side to look him up. He would be at Jackson and Pulaski every day. I told him, "Sure, I'll be there next year. He smiled. I turned over in my bunk, facing the wall, and went to sleep.

It appeared it would take forever to reach Minnesota, but we finally did at about 2:00 in the afternoon. Then it seemed like it was another couple of hours leaving the city part and traveling the country roads to Sandstone Correctional Center. The bus pulled through the side gate, and we were all led into the brick building. It was a brick, country-looking building designed like a city hall or post office on the outside. The buildings were oblong-shaped, two stories, with sections of cells on both sides and both stories. They were sectioned off with sixty inmates to a section. One section was on the north side of the building, and one was on the south side. The galleries were separated by a day room and an office. On the east side of the office, there was a door to the north section, and on the west side of the office, there was a door to the south section. It was set up like this on both floors and all around the complex.

I had been sitting with a guy named Leonard and one named Robinson from Detroit. Leonard was a dark skinned, slender, and nice-looking fellow with a trimmed thin mustache. His hair was cut low to his head, whereas Robinson was a light-skinned guy with curly hair, and he was a prize fighter. Leonard was an electrician by trade, but he and his brother-in-law Robinson were one of Detroit's biggest dope dealers, and that is what they were busted for. They were sentenced to five years apiece.

I liked Leonard, and he had taken a liking to me. So, the three of us were locked in the same cell house and the same dormitory. The beds sat in cubicles and my cubicle was right across from Leonard and Robinson's cubicle. The cubicles stood about four or five feet tall. There was a desk inside the cubicle right across from the bed, and next to that desk, there was a small closet to store your coats and caps in. On one side of the closet, there were three drawers to store your shirts or whatever you wanted to store in them. The cubicle desks and closets were made of metal. The cubicles were designed for a single inhabitant.

We had to wait three days to get assigned to a job. So, during those three days, we found out about all the facilities that were available for us to utilize. There was a library. They had all kinds of sports and games that were available to us. They had pinball and hockey machines. We could play baseball, football, handball, croquet, and volleyball. I loved to play handball and that was enough exercise for me.

This was a country club compared to Statesville. I remember the second day when we had orientation. On a particular day, about 35 of us sat in the orientation room. After about fifteen minutes of being there, the inmates were all talking amongst themselves when a little thin guy with blond hair interrupted our conversations. He had on a gray shirt and a pants set like a work uniform. He said, "Good morning, gentlemen." As he closed the door behind him. He said, "My name is Officer Duckworth, and I will need your attention, gentlemen, for about twenty minutes this morning."

We were all sitting facing the desk as he sat behind it. "Those of you who haven't been to Sandstone before, first of all, let's have a show of hands." "How many of you have been here before?" Three guys raise their hands. "Well, I'm sure you three guys who raided your hands will let your fellow inmates know that this is a correctional center and that we are here to help the inmates, not to harm them." "You can either learn from this experience and enjoy all of the activities that we make available to you, or you can just be a plain asshole and make it hard on yourself." "Now, as you can see when you first came into the compound there are no guards In the tower and the wall itself is only about 11' tall."

If you think you know the way back to these cities of your hometowns, you're welcome to climb these walls. As I said before, there are no guards, but we pay these farmers around $500.00 a head, dead or alive, and they are all crack shots. If they don't get you, you've got a whirlpool up here like quicksand." "This is Minnesota, so, if that doesn't work, the weather will get you and the weather doesn't get you, these wild animals will." "If you're fortunate enough to get away, you'll see Mr. Duckworth knocking on your door." "I know you wouldn't want to see me at your door, would you fellows?" "They also call me the troubleshooting officer." "If any of the fellows have any trouble with other inmates, officers, or the compound, or if you have any trouble at home, put in a request to see Mr. Duckworth." "I'd like to thank you fellows for your attention, and you can line up right here on this wall, then you can go back to your cell house or the yard."

CHAPTER 4

There wasn't any work to be done, I hadn't gotten assigned to a work detail. So, my time was spent in the yard on the handball court or in the library, listening to the penitentiary lawyers arguing among themselves trying everybody's cases except their own. I found that the library was like the "fire barrel." If they weren't crowded up in the library talking about law, they were crowded up in the library talking about the streets, pimping, dope dealing, burglary, robbery, etc.

On a particular day, I sat there listening to the stories that they were telling. There were about ten of us sitting around that day. The size of the library was about 14' by 14'. The other four rooms were used for classes like typing, GED, etc. I wasn't interested in any of those. I was listening to this one guy that they called saucer-mouth Phil. They called him saucer mouth because his lips hung loose, and they were big.

He said, "Yeah man!" "I had a girl who always used to come up short with my money and you know us guys in New York don't play that short money shit." "Therefore, I came up with a remedy, I thought, for the bitch." "You know I had whipped her ass so much that I could feel it myself" "The more I whipped her ass, the more she would shorten my money." "So, I was determined to stop her." Those ass whippings weren't doing the situation any good." "So, I came up with a remedy." "She would come walking her ass up into the house at 1:00 in the afternoon, she had stayed out all night, cut her eyes over at me, and dropped $100.00 on the bed." I said, "I'm not going to whip your today, bitch."

"I told her to get out of her clothes because I was going to give her a bath." "She undressed, but before she reached the house, I had run a quarter of a tub of water for her." "I told her to climb into it." "She did." "I went to the hallway closet and pulled a hundred-pound bag of ice cubes out." "I took it to the bathroom and covered the tub and her with those ice cubes." "I told the bitch I was going to teach her about playing with my money." "Now, you're going to sit in this tub until all of them damn ice cubes melt, or either you can come and face this damn Billy club." "I've been waiting on your black ass." "So, you can make up your mind whether you're going to face that tub or this Billy club." I'm here all day today with you, bitch." "I seated myself in the hallway in front of the bathroom door with the door wide open so that she could see me, and I could look at her."

After twenty minutes she started begging me to let her out of the tub." "Half an hour later, she started crying telling me how cold she was." "Her teeth were chattering now." "She couldn't hardly talk." "Her words were incoherent after about 40 minutes. "She was a dark-skinned girl, pretty in some way, but after 45 minutes she had turned blue." "She promised me the moon." "She promised me that she could never do any of the things that she had been doing." "She cried and swore to God that she would never do those things again." "I thought that she had enough that I had broken her, so, I snatched her out of the tub and dragged her out through the hallway and threw her back ass into that dark closet in the hallway."

"I said, 'I'm being nice to you today, hoe, but the next time you pull anything like you've been doing, I'm going to kill your black ass." 'Do you understand me?" She said, "Yes, in tears." "I took the skeleton key and locked the closet door." "I left the apartment going to check my traps." "I had four or five other whores on the street, plus I had four or five little dealers pitching Riddling and cough syrup." "Most of my pitchers were underage ad making me damn good money." "I didn't give a damn about them getting busted. "If they got busted, I'd get me another one to pitch." "I stayed out about three hours." "I'd given the hoe enough time to think and consider that I wasn't bullshitting with her." "I was sure that I had broken her will."

"Yes, I was sure I had broken her will." "I had about four shots and three or four drags of a good joint and I was high and feeling pretty good." "I was getting ready to show this bitch who was master." "I wasn't going to lecture this bitch anymore." "I was going to let her know exactly how I felt." "I kind of staggered p to the door." "OK, bitch!" I said out loud!' "I hope you learned your damn lesson." "I'm going to let your ass out of the closet." "I opened the door, and that's when I felt the sharp sting." "The blow struck me across the nose and one of my eyes." "It felt like a log had hit me in the eye." "The sting came again harder this time across my lips and jaw." "I threw up my hand and staggered backward, not seeing anything."

"The blow hit me again across the top of my head I felt her body as she ran over me through the hallway." "I fell to the floor." "She ran out of the apartment naked." "Four days later, I was arrested for white slavery because I had brought her from St. Louis." "Plus, all those little dumb boys that I had dealing for me had gotten their mother to press charges against me, and that's how I came up with fifteen years." "The scars haven't healed yet from that bitch's beating she gave me over my head with those clothes hangers she had wrapped together, and the doctor is saying that I might go blind in my right eye." All these problems I'm having come from one no-good hoe." "There are many nights that I wish I had never met her." "I'm telling all you guys today if a woman is for you, there's no better thing, but when she's against you, she is dangerous because she will kill you."

I thought for a long time about what saucer-mouth Phil had said. I thought about Nella. I wondered if she had tried to kill me that night she hit me with the picture lamp. I didn't want to believe it, but deep down in my heart, I knew it was true. I pushed her to the side for a younger girl. Even the police had told me that night she thought she had killed me.

Two months had passed, and the only person I had written to was my mother. In her letters, she said that she hadn't seen my family since I'd been gone. I couldn't go out like Saucer-mouth Phil. My mentors had taught me through the years that once you had a woman, you could always have her again. It all depends on how you come to her.

For the next two or three weeks I kind of stayed to myself, reading good books, and different types of religious books like Muslim, Hindu, and Buddhist books. All those religions had no meaning to me at the time, nor could I understand what they were writing about or trying to convey. I got some poetry books, and I read good poems for about two or three weeks.

The pressure was hard on me, not hearing from Nella. I wanted to hear her voice. I wanted to hear her say "I love you." As the weeks passed, the pressure became worse at night. I remembered the good times that we had, and that little voice reminded me what a stable and caring wife she was. I tossed and turned in my sleep, thinking of her. In the daytime, I was like a zombie walking blindly.

CHAPTER 5

It was about a month and a half into my sentence that I laid up on my bed asking God to help me and show me my mistakes. One of the things that I knew was that I was drinking too much. I asked God to take that away from me but what about Nella, what did I do, where did I go wrong? Maybe I should've thought about the fact that Nella was a woman and therefore she needed me to be there as her man more. I didn't want to be just a good provider, but a good companion to her. She had needs just like I did. I was so busy trying to fail her by providing for her and the kids that I forgot to provide love companionship, friendship, and just being there to share the hardships that she suffered through with the rearing of our kids and caring for them. She didn't have me there at night to help her relieve some of the pressure and stress that she experienced with her days.

I may have added some of that stress because of my long hours of hustling. I left her alone so many nights that she may have felt insecure about our relationship. It may have made her think that I loved someone else and not her. At this point, it seemed like a 9 to 5 job was much better for a husband, but I didn't like that. I didn't know anything about working set hours like in an office. I was a hustler and that's all I knew and that's all I do and that's where the conflict would come in.

I knew I needed Nella and the kids because they are part of me too. Without them, there's nothing. I had to find a way to have time to spend with Nella and the kidsl and still be able to hustle. I knew that it would work because Nella was very understanding and patient. I knew that she knew that I wouldn't be able to be home early every night but at least once a week I should be home with my family, and I knew this. My thoughts kept going on and, on every day, thinking about Nella then one day out of the clear blue sky the mailman called out my name.

I went to the men's washroom with my letter and sat in a stall with the door locked. I began to take the letter out of the envelope. The letter began, "Well man, I guess you are settled now after these 60 days." "I saw your mother last week." "Well, as far as I'm concerned, I have no guilty conscience of your being there." "At first I had malice in my heart about your little girlfriend, but I guess if you love her the way that I have loved you through the years you all deserve to be together." "As far as myself, I'm going to let God lead me to my next companion and I hope that this companion will be in love with me." "I wish you well."

I sat there for a while; my whole understanding was messed up. I thought about the way that she had taken care of me through the years. I thought about the way that she had stuck by me and now she's talking about giving her love to another nigger and there was nothing I could do about it but lay here and do this year. Mr. Buddie's words came back to me when I tried to learn how to shine those shoes as he did, and I kept messing up. Hitting the men's toes and putting shoe polish all over their socks when I tried to brush their shoes. Mr. Buddy said, "Al, nothing beats a failure but a try."

LIFE OF A HUSTLER IN CHICAGO

"When you fail, try again and try again." Keep trying until you suc- ceed." "You'll get the grip of that brush just keep trying."

Waddell's words also came back to me, "If you ever had a woman for some time, you could always cop her again with the same manner that you had copped her before, that is if she was in love with you." I knew what I had to do. I had to get Nella's mind out of this mode that it was now in and set her mind in another direction. So, I came out of the bathroom and went straight to my cubicle. Certain guys in the hallway spoke to me. I met Jake near my cubicle. He said, "Al, we're fixing to play some Wisk." "Johnson and Len are going to be partners." "Do you want to be my partner?" "We're going to play for cigarettes, two packs a game." He faced me and I looked him in the eyes. He said, "What's wrong, man?" He could see the tears in my eyes. I said, "You're my man, Jake, and I wouldn't tell anybody this but you." "I also want you to know that I'm a big boy now and I can handle it, but I just got a 'Dear John letter' from the sweetest woman in the world." He asked, "Your wife?" I said "Yes." He said, "Man, you told me about that other woman, is this what she said?" I said, "Yes, in so many words." He said, "Man, she's just pulling your leg, man, she ain't left, you man."

She just wants you to suffer from that bullshit that you whipped on her." "She wants you to think about it." "She wants to hurt your black ass as you hurt her." "So, you know what you've got to do now, little brother." "You've got to get that pad out and put that pen in your hand and tell her his ain't the way it's going to go." "This is the way it's going to go!" I said, "That's exactly what I was going to do when you stopped me." He said, "OK, I'll tell you what." "I'm going to get a substitute to play with me, and when you get through with that bad letter that I know you're going to write, you can come on out." I said, "OK, and I went into my cubicle."

It was three hours later that I had finished the letter to Nella, I had put the stamp on the envelope, but you weren't allowed to seal it. I gave the letter to the officer to mail out for me. I went into the bathroom and washed up and went back to my cubicle and changed into clean jeans and a white tee shirt. I put on my black house shoes and tied a black head rag tight on my head. It was Friday, and there was no work the next day. Jake was waiting for me. I made my way to the dayroom.

The big room was crowded with some looking at the TV, some inmates were playing dominoes, and some were playing cards on three different tables. The table that Jake was at sat in the middle of the room. I made it there. I looked at Jake and said, "How many are we down, partner, or are we up? He said, "We're up eight packs." I thanked the fellow who was playing with Jake. I said, "I'll take over now, partner." "You've got two packs coming in the morning." The next week I hung out in the library from 8:00 until lunchtime at 11:30.

In the library, I read books, heavy books, I thought about Plato, Aristotle, and Niche. Platonism about the Greeks and their philosophy. I read about Hinduism and Buddhism, and I read about Muhammad. All the religions were confusing because I was so hooked on Jesus Christ that I did not even try to understand the theological meaning that they were based on. As I drove myself deeper into books, two weeks had gone by and there was no answer from Nella. I found myself getting weak from the thought of her. On that third week, I wrote her again, begging her for forgiveness and telling her how much I loved her. "Please forgive me," I asked her in the letter.

I kept reading up in the afternoons after lunch. I would either go and play handball or go right back to that library, reading law books, reading anything that would satisfy the mind. It was the sixth week that I heard from Nella. She was mostly telling me that my kids were fine. She hadn't seen my mother, but she felt that they were doing fine as well. I began to write her longer letters, promising promises. Promising on top of the promise that I would straighten up, and that she was the only person in the world that I loved. I never loved anyone like I loved her. Please, baby, give me one more chance at happiness with you and my kids. These words didn't seem to matter to her. She started taking a longer time to answer my letters. Her letters had no meaning and no love in them. They were cold.

After being at Sandstone for five months and not getting my business straight with Nella, I started getting weaker in spirit, and my stomach had that knot in it that I couldn't relieve. They had started me to work in the glove factory. There, you make a little change a month. They did this to other inmates whose families weren't sending them any money. I didn't seem to be able to understand the sewing machine, so I wasn't putting out any gloves. I seemed to always be in a daze. I was walking around in a cloud.

On a particular day, we were all coming back into the factory, where sewing machines were lined up in rows. I was number 36. As I made my way across the aisle to go to my machine, I slipped and came down hard on the concrete. Almost passing out, I could barely see the blood that shot from my nose. Later, as I recovered, I was in the hospital with a bandage around my head. I looked around the room, and there were two other patients. There was a black guy who had on green hospital pajamas. He kind of waved his hand to me and told me that his name was Charles. He pointed at the white guy who had his leg tied up in the air in a sling. "This is Rick." Rick said, "Hi to me and went back to reading his book. I said to them, "Hi fellows, my name is Al Wynn." Charles said, "We thought you were a goner, man, when you first came in here." "What did the doctors say that you have, a concussion?"

The most we did every day in that hospital was listen to music on headphones. The more music I listened to, the more depressed I got. I had less than six months left to serve before my sentence would be over. I could never get Nella to tell me that she loved me in her letter. So, if that's the game that she wanted to play, I thought, then we both could play it.

Charles and Rick had left. Newcomers were coming in and going out of the hospital. They would come in for a couple of days and then leave. Me, I was glad to be there, no work and it gave me time to think. There was one guy named Nelson, he was from the west side of Chicago and had been there for four days. He said, "Well, Al, what are you going to do when you get out, you're getting short, aren't you? I said, "Yes, less than four months, and when I first get out, I'm going to get me a contracting shop." "I did tell you I was a contractor, didn't I?" He said "Yeah." I said, "Man, I used to make all kinds of money." "I'm going to get out of here and get me a contractor's office, a sissy with a white poodle, and a convertible helicopter." He started cracking up, and I laughed with him. I said, "I was joking, man." He said, "Yeah, I know." I said, "But for real, I'm going to get that office, a Cadillac, and the prettiest lady in Chicago."

I told him that my wife wants to play games with me, so I'm going to show her how to play. He said, "What did she do, Al, have you locked up?" I said, "Yes, and quit my black ass when I got here," He said, "Yeah, man, I know, that's some cold shit, there. He asked me, "Do you still love her?" I said, "To be true to myself more than ever, but I'm fixing to teach her black ass a lesson like she's doing to me." Before long, Nelson had slipped off to sleep. I grabbed the pen and reached and got the pad, and I wrote:

Dear Nella, Time is not as long as it has been and not as short as it's going to get. I can tell at this time that you have found someone that you care for because of the way you've been writing to me, I know that your love is gone and I know that I can't find a defense for the way I've hurt you but as I told you years ago I have enjoyed every second moment hour, and day that I have shared with you and I just hope when I come home that I can find someone that as worthy as you have been. The fellow that you have met is very lucky, and now that I see the light. I wish you well.

For the next four or five months, I read books and the Bible, and I concentrated every day and dreamed of the things I needed and wanted, such as the office, the Cadillac, and the woman. I could visualize myself having all these things when I got home. A person does not understand the mystery of the mind, the mystery of God, or the mystery of God's words. I was soon to grasp a better understanding of them all. Like the meaning of faith, *"Faith is the substance of a thing heard of, and the evidence of a thing not seen that reaches out into the unknown and takes a hold of that which is not until it becomes that which is."* I always thought that was a heavy saying there, very, very, very deep. The days and weeks passed, and I was finally released.

CHAPTER 6

It was August of 1967, and the Black Stone Rangers were going crazy, shooting people. A boy got blown away on the bus by the Black Stone Rangers. The onlookers on the bus said that his whole head was blown off with a shotgun. They were taking over the Southmoore Hotel. Their headquarters were 67th and Blackstone. The neighborhood was fearful of what they might do next. All the gangs had started extorting and killing people. Chicago was becoming a nightmare. The elderly people stayed at home, staying off the streets at night. Most elderly people's sons were a part of the night stalkers, and if those sons rebelled against the gang, then they would get beaten up or killed. There were no daddies or brothers who would help them or save them, so they had to become a part of the gang.

I was fortunate enough to stay in the hospital until my time was up, so they sent me home on a two-passenger airplane, and that was a hell of an experience. We were so far up in the air that when the police agent showed me the Mississippi River, it looked like a piece of string. That was my first flight and my last one. I prayed to God that if I got down from there safely, I promised that I would never fly again, and I have never flown again. My brother, Robert, met me at Midway Airport. He took me straight to my mother's house when I was still on Morgan. My mother had left me a brand-new suit and $200.00. I met my brother's wife. He got married while I was away. After dressing, I tried my best to stick around to see Gloria, but after a while, I called a cab and headed for the house of Nelson on 65th and Cottage Grove to get my hair done.

I had gotten Nella's address from my brother, and after getting my hair done, I headed straight for her apartment, which was located on 73rd and Dorchester. After I arrived at the apartment, Nella was out, but all the kids were happy to see me, even her oldest daughter, who was babysitting the rest of the children. I found that Nella had a job working for her father as a hostess at the Living Room Lounge, which her father had bought. I didn't want to create any disturbance, so I did not go to The Living Room Lounge, instead, I caught a cab to 47th Street. I stopped in the Family Affair Lounge and peeped into Chili Mac's on 47th Street, a chili parlor. I hit two or three more lounges on 47th Street before I started getting tipsy.

By 10:30 that night, I ended up at Joe's house. Her husband, Norman, and her brother, Heno, were happy to see me and were glad that I was home. I was in the kitchen with Joe as she was fixing a plate for me. I asked Joe if I could give her $100,00 to stay a couple of days. She said, "Sure, you can, and if that's all the money that you've got, you can pay me later." I sat at the table eating my food. I heard Joe in the dining room by the bar talking to her husband, Norman. "Baby, Al, wants to crash with her for a couple of days." "He wanted to pay me, but I didn't want to take his money." "He could sleep on the couch if it's alright with you. He said, "Sure, he can stay."

The next couple of days, I reacquainted myself with the neighborhood. I found Calvin, Harvey, and Billy, all of them under the L station tracks on 47th Street. They were all more than happy to see me after I had chipped in and bought about three or four pints of gin. Harvey pulled me to the side and said, "Al, you know that old big-legged girl that used to live in that project that you lived in on 48th and State, what's her name, Lu?" I said, "You are talking about Lucinda." He said, "Yeah, that's who I'm talking about." "She lived up there on the 6th floor." I said, "Yeah, I know her." "Is she still married?" He said, "Yeah, I see that old guy she's married to." I talk to her in the tavern, and he acts like she's his sister or something." "Yeah, they all act like that." "What kind of man is that, Al?" "Yeah, as pretty as Lucinda is if I were her husband, I'd hit everybody in the head that tried to talk to her." I said, "Yeah, man, she's nice-looking, uh, what's happening? He said, "I just wanted to tell you, man, she said she's crazy about you and can hardly wait for you to get home, and when I see you, tell you to make it there to her."

"I remember that night that you first introduced her to me up at that Pony Keg Lounge up on 51st and King Drive, but I thought you had just met her man." I said, "No, Lucinda and I have been friends ever since I first moved into the projects, but it was so close to home that I didn't hang around too tough." "That husband at that time wasn't too understanding, either, especially with me."

That evening, I left Harvey in the crowd under the L station, still drinking. I caught a cab on King Drive to the Pony Keg Lounge. Bill Lowe was the bartender and a good friend of Cinda's. The place was crowded. I sat at the end of the bar. Bill was at the other end. He had two bartenders working at the bar. I didn't know the other guy, but he poured my Gin Fizz. It was about 15 or 20 minutes before Bill caught my eye. He smiled and rushed over to me. "Al, Al, Al, my man!!" I said, "What's happening, Bill?" He said, "What else can be happening with a bartender but work?" He said, "I can't do shit anymore, eyeing this bar every day." We talked small talk.

I told him I had done a year for that check that the police were looking for me for." I said, "I'm clean now." "I'm just trying to get back some of the things I lost." I said, "By the way, have you seen your girl?" He said, "You're talking about that crazy, Lucinda?" I said, "Yeah, you got her number?" He said, "Yeah." I said, "Give it to me." He brought the number back and placed the business phone in front of me. I dialed her number, and she answered the phone. I said, "Hi, pretty!" She said, "Al, Al Wyn!" I said, "Yeah, this is me." She said, "Tell me you're out, you're not calling me from no damn jail." I said, "Yeah, I'm oat the Pony Keg." Where's that damn husband of yours? She said he's at work and wouldn't get off until 8:00 in the morning. He's a security guard for Al Abrahams, the car dealer on 47th Street. I said, "How long will it take you to get here?" She said, "Give me an hour." I said, "Cool."

Lucinda and I drank for a couple of hours there with Bill, and then we slipped to the corner of the Zanzibar and rented a room. I cried out all my sorrows to her. I told her that good stuff, like if I weren't married, she would be the only girl that I would marry. "I hold something real deep in my heart for you, baby," I told her. But you know me and we kind of understand each other, don't we?" I told her, "I enjoy myself when I'm with you." "You're like a fulfill-ment every time I see you.," She said, "Yeah, Al, I understand you. I understand you more than you think I do," reaching over and getting her cigarettes from the table and lighting one.

I looked up at her at the nakedness of her well-rounded breast as she sat up in bed with her small waist and her bulging hips showing from under the sheet. She puffed on the cigarette. She said, "I want you to know, Al, you're not the only one getting fulfillment." "I wouldn't be here if you weren't doing the same thing for me, baby." I said, "Tell me something, do you or your husband have any money lying around that you aren't using right now?" She said, "No, not real money." "I just got my brother out of trouble for shooting a guy over on Champlain the other night." "I'm kind of knocked."

"What do you need?" I said, "Well, you know I just got out and I don't even have a change of drawers, and I need a little money for a band to try and make some money." "I've been running around in that suit for two days, maybe I can as my auntie and see what she can do for me." She said, "Baby, I don't have any money, if I did you know you can get my heart if you want it, but I do have a credit card." "Maybe you can meet me at Max's Clothing there by the L station at about 1:00," I said, "Yes, darling, I can wait that long."

CHAPTER 7

I left Max's Clothing with a couple of matching shirts and pantsuits, a couple of slacks and matching sweaters, and a couple of pairs of Stacy Adams. Joe had met Lucinda a couple of times, and she stood there in her living room admiring the gifts that Lucinda had bought me. She said, "Al, you're something else!" "That girl loves you. She told me while you were away that she doesn't give a damn about her husband. I said, "Yeah, Joe all women say they're in love until you say something wrong or step on their toes then they want to shoot your ass or put you in jail like Nella just did to me. "So, I just take all of that as if they're blowing smoke up my ass and keep going." Joe was like her mother, Cousin Callie, sold breakfast, and dinners, rented rooms when her husband was off at work, and sold liquor at her bar. Our conversation was interrupted by the buzzing of the doorbell. It was three of her drinking customers.

They entered the room and headed for the bar. Joe introduced me to them, two men and a lady. Ralph, Lewis, and Connie. I bowed my head to each of them and continued to place my clothes in the hallway closet. I went into the bathroom, took a shower, and changed into one of my new outfits. The people at the bar were having great fun, laughing and talking among themselves with Joe behind the bar drinking with them. I entered the room and just for a moment, Connie and my eyes locked. Then I shifted my attention to Joe. I said, "I'm sorry, but I'm fixing to leave. "I should be back about midnight tonight." She said, "Be careful out there." I said, "I will," and I left.

I headed straight for the Democratic Hall on 46th and Prairie, two or three doors from Glady's Restaurant, which was in the basement. There were five or six guys shooting dice there, it wasn't too crowded. So, I hung around there for about two hours betting on the cinch bets that don't come, don't make, don't bar. I had about $150.000 in my pocket when I first got there. When I left, I had about $250.00, and I made about $100.00.

I caught a jitney to the 411 Club on 63rd Street. Everyone who knew me was happy to see me. I shook hands and bought drinks, and they bought me drinks. It was about 9:30 at night that I got up nerve enough to call Mrs. Clark. She answered the phone. I said, "Hello, baby!" I said, "This is Al." She said, "Al Wynn?" I said, "Yes." She said, "Well, Al," in kind of an explanatory way, "If you are calling about the car, I let it go back." "I heard about your misfortune and I'm sorry that it happened that way for you." "Of course, I went back to my husband." "He's not here now, he drives a cab at night." "You will always be my friend, Al." "I hold something very dear for you in my heart, but I wish that you wouldn't call this number again." "By the way, Al, if you haven't heard, Leona died five months ago." "I was at her funeral." "You take care of yourself, goodnight!"

That next week, I gambled, saw Lucinda from time to time, and got a couple of dollars from her. It had been about sixteen or seventeen days since I had been out of jail. I sat at the bar talking to Joe and sipping a Budweiser beer when the telephone rang. Joe went to answer it, and she hollered back to me, "Al, telephone." She handed me the phone, and as she handed me the phone, she said,

"It's your wife, Nella." My heart starts pounding. I said, "Hello." She said, "Hello, Al." I said, "Hello, how are you doing?" She said, "I'm doing fine." "Have you been out here today?" I said, "Out here, where?" I asked her, "Out to my house?" I replied, "No, I haven't been out there." She said, "Well, your oldest daughter isn't here, and I thought maybe you had her with you." I said, "No!" She said, "She hasn't made it home from school yet, and she's never been this late getting home from school before." "I guess I'll go back out and see if I can find her." I said, "If you want me to, I'll come out there." She said, "You can come on, I'll be here." I caught a jitney to 72nd and Backstone.

CHAPTER 8

When I arrived, Nella let me in, and my daughter, Christine, was in the kitchen washing dishes. All the kids were happy to see me. My wife sat on her couch, sipping on her beer, kind of looking at me admiringly. I said, "So, the lost sheep came home?" She said, "Yeah, she went with one of her girlfriends to the football game." Nella and I sat on that couch and drank beer and some gin she had for about two hours. We laughed and talked about old times. It was about 8:30 when the children came back into the house. My daughter said, "Daddy, are you staying, are you coming back home?" My son said, "Yeah, Daddy, are you coming back home?" My wife said, "Yeah, he's staying, can't you see he's too drunk to go anywhere and it's about time that he came back home."

Nella told me, "Your kids miss you, man, and I do, too." My daughter said, "Aren't you going to show him the present that you got him?" My wife got up and went to the closet and brought back a beautiful gray suit, went into her dresser drawer, and gave me an envelope." She said, "I've been saving this since you went away.," She said, "I know you don't have a job now so, spend it carefully." I opened the envelope, and there was $500.00 in it. The next week I moved all my stuff back home from Joe's house. Joe, my mother, sister, and brother were glad that I went back home.

For the next two or three weeks, the only thing I did was rest, dress, get drunk, and explore the neighborhood. My wife had warned me about 67th and Stony Island. The Blackstone Rangers and even the neighborhood we lived in were dangerous. She told me to be very careful. So, I stayed out of the reach of the gang bangers. I found out where the older men went to date and have fun. The older men consisted of the city's garbage truck drivers, the mailmen, and the policemen. They all gathered at the Black Marble Lounge at 69th and Stony Island. I hung out mostly in the Stony Liquor and Lounge on the other corner of 69th Street.

Two weeks had passed, and I had only $5.00 left out of the $500.00 my wife had given me, and I was drunk and outdoors trying to make it home from Stony Liquors. I had on that grey suit that my wife had bought me with a grey Boseleni hat with a big black band. I wore a tie with a white shirt. I staggered myself down the street, headed for 72nd and Stony. The Stony Liquors sat on the corner of 69th Street on the north side. I staggered to the south side corner of the front of the Black Marble Lounge. I kind of hesitated in front of the Black Marble Liquors and continued staggering on down trying to reach the next corner.

The next storefront after the Black Marble was the cleaners. The cleaners had four storefronts. I had passed the cleaners, and the next storefront had a big sign in the window saying: "FOR RENT." I stopped there and looked at the sign again that said, "FOR RENT." I looked at the door again, the number said 6916. I read the sign again at the bottom, it said, if you want to see the inside get the key from the cleaners next door. I kind of straightened myself up and checked my tie in the window glass of the storefront, kind of pulled my hat down tight on my head and after I thought I had gotten myself together, I kind of braced myself and went into the cleaners for the keys.

I went to the counter of the cleaners and asked the girl. She called out to her boss, "Opy!" "Three's a man up here that wants to see the storefront next door." "I'll be there in a minute," he said. After a while a man about 6'5: weighing about 450 lbs came to the counter with the key. He said, "You want to follow me next door?" I said, "OK," and we went next door. We were inside the place in the front office about 9'X 8' with a tile ceiling and tile floor. Missing tiles were on the ceiling and the floor. Dirty curtains were around the windows and the door glass. He opened the door that led to the back of the storefront.

The store was deep in size, and in front of the store, on the wall next to the cleaners, there were several large holes as if someone had kicked holes in the drywall. The floor was filled with cracks, and it seemed as if there were three or four pieces of rotten flooring. The bathroom sat way back in the right corner in the rear of the room. There was an old-fashioned sink that leaked. There was a toilet with a twisted toilet seat, the toilet door was old-fashioned with no knob. The rear door had two 3X4s across it acting as a lock. There were scaly ceilings and walls. He said, "Well, do you like it?" I said, "Yeah, it can be made into something."

He said, "If you want the place, we can go next door and call the owner." We headed for the telephone. Opy had the telephone up to his ear now, Bill Crust, he told the operator on the other end. He waited for a minute or two. "Mr. Crust," he said, "I have a gentleman here who wants to rent the place next door at 6916 Stony Island." "We would like to talk to him?" Opy turned towards me and handed me the phone. I took the phone. I said, "Mr. Crust, my name is Al Wynn, and I would like to rent the store next door if the rent is not too much. He said, "Well, if you're interested, it's about 12:39. I'm going to lunch now." "So, if you're interested, you can come down here to see me." I said, "Yes, I'll be there."

There was no need to go home now, it was going on about 12:45. So, I walked back to Stony Liquors, went into the men's room, and washed my face three times in cold water. Then I went to the front of the bar and ordered some breath mints, caught the bus on the east side of 69th Street, and took the train downtown, I sat on the train in an empty car. I sat in the conductor's compartment with my eyes closed as though I was trying to catch a nap before I reached the loop. What the hell was I doing? I questioned myself. It appears I had a forcible will driving me to an unknown destination with just carfare there and back, what the hell was the purpose of my going? I didn't have another dime in my pocket other than the carfare and I didn't know any other place to get some money from and I didn't have a job, what the hell was I doing going downtown, but I was on my way, so, I might as well play it out.

I went to the fourth floor of the Pan Am Building, and as I stepped off the elevator, I almost fell from ducking when I saw a huge model plane that hung over my head and was pointing at the elevator. I imagine that people familiar with the Pan Am building were used to seeing the model plane but me being new to the building it gave me a scare as I looked to the right of me at the big giant glass wall that stretched from one end of the floor to the other end, I noticed the secretary sitting behind the two glass door that led into the office.

On the east side of her desk was a glass door that read American Real Estate Co., and on the west side was another glass door that read Benton's Distillery Company. Four-foot benches and chairs sat in front of each door with their back up against the glass wall. After telling her my purpose for being there she told me to have a seat in front of the real estate door. She called Mr. Crust, "There's an Al Wynn out here to see you." She looked over at me and said, "He'll be here shortly." I thanked her. I sat uncomfortably staring at the ceiling and the wall and wishing that I had a drink to relax me from my nervousness. In about ten minutes, a huge man about 6'1" tall and weighing about 220 lbs. with solid blond hair and dressed very neatly in a black pin-striped suit, came out of the office. "Mr. Wynn?" he asked me. I said, "Yes." "Bill Crust." He said. He held the door open and asked me to come in. It was a huge room with about 50 desks lined up in rows, 50 typewriters, and 50 secretaries sitting behind them. None of them seemed to notice me.

Across the room, I could see a double glass sliding door, and it seemed the room was filled with typewriters and secretaries. Mr. Crust led me into the 1st room to the left of the door. The room was spacious. On the east wall, it had shelves about 8' to 10' long with all brands of whiskey lining all the shelves. It had what seemed like a 10' long table in the middle of the floor with fifths of whiskey on it. Paper cups and plastic glasses sat on the end of the table. A black leather couch with no back to it stretched out the length of the table on the west side of the room. Mr. Crust's desk sat about 4' from the end of the table. It was a big desk with a big swivel chair that seemed to be made just for a man his size.

"You have to excuse me for a moment, Mr. Wynn, I have some papers that must be finished for the girl, and I'll be with you in a moment." He reached for a pen and started writing on some paper. He seemed to be deep in thought as he was writing. About three or four minutes later, he looked up at me again. "Mr. Wynn, as you can see, this is a real estate office and a distillery co. combined, and it keeps me busy as hell. "You drink, Mr. Wynn?" I said, "Occasionally." "Well, if you see anything here help yourself to it. "I have to run this on the other side there," and he left. About a minute after he left, I got one of those plastic glasses, poured almost a glass of Green Leaf Vodka, and guzzled it down. It's a wonder that I didn't have a heart attack on the spot the way I guzzled it down. Then I poured another shot or two into the glass and sat back down. It wasn't too long before he returned to the room and was sitting behind his desk.

"Now, let's see, Mr. Wynn, let's see." He was reaching for a big book on his desk and looking through it until he found the page he wanted. He asked me, "Did you see the place, Mr. Wynn? did you go in there?" "Yes, I did," I replied while taking little sips of vodka. "Well, did you notice that we just had central air put in thee, did you notice that?" I said, "Not particular, I didn't see that." He said, "Well, we just had it done and it was renting for $285.00 per month, and now we want $385.00 a month and we want one-month rent and two months of advance rent, and we give one-year leases."

As he was talking, I stood up with my hat in my hand, showing the label of the hat. He asked me, "So, what do you think, Mr. Wynn?" As he was looking up at me, and saw me standing. "Well, I think I shouldn't take up any more of our time, Mr. Crust," I told him. "No disrespect to you, Mr. Crust, but I think that's a little more than I can chew off. "I mean, I came here thinking that maybe we can make a deal on the place. "When was the last time you saw the place, Mr. Crust?" "About six months ago." He answered, Just before they put the central air into the place."

"Well, then you must have seen the wall right next to the cleaner, how they have kicked holes in the wall and damaged most of the drywall. "The bathroom is in disarray." "Did you notice the rotten wood on the floor in the back?" "You need a new door in the rear with a lock and key, instead of boards nailed on it." "You need the whole place exterminated, scraped, and painted, and not to speak of the front office, you need to throw out all of the curtains that you have around the front windows, tile the floors, and retile the ceiling." He sat there looking at me with a serious look on his face. I went on talking as though I was on a stage "You see, Mr. Crust, I came here because I haven't had a job in four or five months." "I need an office for my type of business, I have been working out of my home. " "I have been doing contracting work for about fifteen years." "So, when I saw the place there at 6916 Stony Island and saw what a wreck it was, I thought it would be a hell of an opportunity for me to show a gentleman like you my hidden talents. "After I was finished with the job, I thought maybe we could reach terms on the rent." "At present, Mr. Crust, you're asking me for $1,000.00, which I don't have." "So, I don't want to take up too much of your time, maybe if I get a couple of jobs under my belt, we can talk further." I turned to leave.

He said, "Just a moment, Mr. Wynn, maybe we can do some business." "You go back and tell Opy that I said to give you the key and you go in and let me know the price that you can fix the place up for. And call me with the price." I thanked him and left. I thanked God back to 69 and Stony Island. I had just gotten my first contracting office. I entered the cleaners' and spoke to Opy about the key. He looked at me and kind of frowned and went straight to the phone. I heard him ask Mr. Crust, "Do you want me to give this fellow the key to next door?" The answer must've been yes because he said, "Very well, I'll take care of it." And hung up the phone.

I knew going out the door that I had the place to do whatever I wanted to do with it because there were two words that I was listening for that I did not hear. One of them was when I talked to Mr. Crust and the key, but he did not tell me to return it to the cleaners. The other one is when Opy talked to Mr. Crust, he didn't tell him to get the key back from me, which gave me enough time to do what I wanted to do, and I knew just what to do to get that storefront. I went home and shared my good news with my family.

CHAPTER 9

It was the weekend, and I rested, not even getting out of bed. I outlined in my mind what I had to do to lock up or secure that place for myself. Mr. Crust had asked me to call him when I got a price. That was my first opportunity. I wasn't going to call him until I did the work and finished it. Only two things could happen if I did that. Either he would just renege period and not pay me because he didn't OK the job and took back his key. That was the worst thing he could do, or he could go along with my price and let me rent it out using the money that he owed me for the rent, and that's the way I wanted him to do it.

That Saturday evening, I called my mother and asked her if I could have a $150.00 loan and that I would pay it back to her double within 30 days. She sent my brother, Robert, over with the money that Sunday. It was Monday, now 8:00 in the morning. I dressed casually for the occasion and walked to 70th and Dorchester to the lounge, which sat on the northwest corner. Several people were standing in front of the lounge, ladies and I. I peeped into the lounge because the door was ajar. A 5-counter that was used for packaging goods was in the front of the lounge by the door. The lounge had about 20 bar stools lining the front of the counter. Two or three tables sat on the opposite wall, with just two chairs at each table. It was a hole-in-the-wall bar with a bathroom that sat in the rear in the left corner.

I continued my walk to the alley. I knew exactly what I was looking for and it sat on the other side of the alley in the vacant lot. About four or five to six people were sitting around it. Some were sitting on liquor crates, and some were sitting on an old, dead tree stump, but it sat there empty and dead-looking. Of course, it would look like this in the summertime. The fire barrel was always dead in the summertime, but it came alive in the winter. I noticed a young boy who seemed to be about twenty years old. He had on a sweater, blue jeans, and combat boots with half his pants down in the boots, and his boots were unlaced. I went over closer to him.

I met Jesse at the Stony Liquor Lounge a couple of weeks ago. We drank most of the day together. I told him some parts of my life on 47th Street and I further told him that I was new to this neighborhood. He said, "You're in luck because I know everybody in this neighborhood." "I was born in this neighborhood, and I work as a mechanic down on Dorchester." "So, if you ever need anything come to see me." I looked over at the garage at the corner of the alley. One door was open with a car sticking out of it, and the other garage door was closed. I kind of figured in my mind that it was the garage that Jesse had described, but I played dumb for the young boy. "Say, my man," I said as I came closer to him. He looked up at me and I said, "Pardon me, do you know a guy by the name of Jesse?" He said, "Jesse, who, my man?" I said, "I don't know his last name." "He did say he was a mechanic." He said, "You must be talking about Mr. Sheet." He looked over at the garage and shouted out, "Hey, Mr. Sheet, Jesse!" A loud voice came out of the garage and said, "Yes!" "A fellow is looking for you!" "Bring your ass on out here!"

Within minutes, the way the car was jacked up in the alley you could see the feet sticking out from under the car. After a while, Jesse slid out on a dolly. He got up and walked towards us. I said, "Hi, Jesse!" He said, "My man, Al!" "How are you doing?" He was close to me and the young boy. I said, "Ma'am, you said if I ever need you to call on you, and I need you today." "Yeah, man, I just copped a storefront up there at 6918 Stony Island." "I told you that I was a contractor." He said, "Yeah, yeah, you did." I told him, "The only difference between me and a real contractor is that the real contractor has money and I'm dead broke. But I've got a little money to try and do what I need to do, and that's the reason that I'm coming to you. I need someone who knows about plastering, painting, a little carpentry, and some plumbing. I don't need a professional because I could show them what to do." "Man, are you drinking?" "Yeah, are you buying?" I said, "Yeah, is this your boy here? He said, "This is Howard. "Howard, this Al." I said, "What are you drinking?" He said, "Man, I'm with the party." I said, "I don't know, man, what about some Mist?" "Do you all drink mist?" He said, "I told you I'm with the party, if you want to drink some panther piss, I'm with you." Jesse said, "Man, Mist is good." I went into my pocket and came out with a twenty. I looked at the young boy. I said, "Man, you want to do the honors?" He said, "Yeah, I'll go and get it." I said, "Yeah, man, I need somebody who will work for a little money." "I'll probably pay them better later on when I get on my feet."

"You know how it is in a new neighborhood." "I need somebody who won't have anybody just walking in the door, who doesn't know me." He said, "Well, my man, this little young boy who you just sent to the store is cool with me." "I go with his sister; his name is Howard." "He's a little Blackstone Ranger, but he's cool." "He will go along with you, he will do whatever I ask him to do, and I'm going to ask him to help you, Mr. Wynn." I said, "Cool!"

Howard was now back, and Jesse filled him in on some of the details we had talked about. As the bottle went up in the air from one person to another, the people started gathering around the bottle. I kind of sipped off the whiskey myself, and I played my hand close to my chest. When I sent Howard for that second fifth, I became the hero of the day and Robin Hood. Everybody loved Al Wynn. At the end of the day, Howard had recruited two more of his friends to help paint my place for only $20.00 apiece, and I'd buy lunch and drinks. It was going to be a party the next day. A working party. Jesse had sent Howard up the alley to recruit Mr. Smith, who was an old plasterer, carpenter, and plumber. Mr. Smith took a drink out of the bottle, looked at me, and said, "I'm not going to stick you up, but I'll be over here tomorrow to take a look at those holes in the wall and see what we can do for that bathroom." He said, "I'll be there." The day had proven itself to be beneficial to me, I thought as I staggered my way home.

CHAPTER 10

t was fun the next day, snatching them off dirty curtains off the windows and doors. I had bought two-fifths of wine Richards Wild Irish Rose Wine. Howard and his guys were having fun in the back of the store painting. They were sipping the wine and singing some of Smokey Robinson's and Marvin Gaye's songs. I knew from a long time ago, "When in Rome, do as the Romans do. So, I sipped the wine. I felt good, and I harmonized with Howard and his group.

On this 2nd day on the job, as we were finishing up the painting, plastering, and plumbing, the guys accepted me as one of their own. Even Mr. Smith showed his affection for me. "Anytime you have any other work you need to be done, call on me. I'm not going to stick you up," he said as I paid him $45.00 for the plastering, plumbing, and carpentry work that he had done on the back door and the floor. He picked up his old rusty suitcase-like bag, which he kept his tools in. He said, "OK, you guys, Howard, I'll see you later and he walked out of the back door, walking home.

I pulled Howard to the side and said, "Here, man, here's another $20.00 a piece for you and your guys, and here's $10.00 to go next door and er another taste. "Get your boy over there, Leroy to go for you," Howard called Leroy to go next door and get a fifth of Mist.

Leroy was a skinny, light-skinned guy with a bald head that showed a scar on the back. He had a comical personality, he liked to tell jokes all the time, and he walked with that hip walk as he walked out of the door for drinks. Melvin, another friend of Howard's, was gathering the empty paint cans and taking them to the alley. I said, "Well, man, you all did a nice job." "This dark gray paint on the wall and this black paint on the floor did wonders to this place."

"Now, all I have to do is tile the ceiling and floors in the front office." I said, "There isn't too much money around here until I get some jobs, but you're welcome to come around here and help me out until I get on my feet, just you." He said, "Yeah, man, I'll go along with that." "What time would you want me to come?" I said, "9:00 is good." We sat around for about another hour and a half talking and drinking that Mist, and then we each went our ways.

Howard was a slim 6' tall young man, about 22 years old, weighed about 180 lbs., had long arms, and was nice looking. I could feel him moving towards me, offering friendship. First, I needed that friendship because of his age group and because he belonged to that gang, and secondly, I needed a backup around me to cover my back, but Howard didn't know he had just been recruited by me.

CHAPTER 11

After finishing the place, I played around in it for a week, keeping it open and drinking in the back of the shop with certain friends I had met at Stony Liquors and the Black Marble Lounge. I didn't allow the younger crowd in there, only Howard and a couple of his friends. One day, as Howard and I were sitting in the front office, I sat at the old desk that was left in place, and Howard sat on a stool. We were drinking beers when a tap came at the window, Howard went to the door and peeped out of the window. He said, "It's one of my friends, Bullwhip." "Can I let him in or do you want me to step outside and talk to him?" I told him, "You can let him in."

As Bullwhip entered the door, Howard introduced him to me as "Bullwhip." "But we all call him Bull," Howard said, "And Bull, this is Mr. Wynn, Al Wynn." Bull bowed his head and reached his hand out to me, and I shook it. He turned his attention back to Howard and said, "Man, I saw you in, do you got a $1.00 or something, I need a beer, I need a drink or something." "It's been a bad day for me." "I can't hustle upon nothing." I had about four six-packs of beer in the back, in the refrigerator. I said, "Do you need a beer, man?" He said, "Yeah, I could stand a drink." I told Howard to go into the back and get a 6 pack.

We sat around, just the three of us drinking. I told them mostly about my younger life. Young boys love to talk about pimping and hustling. They liked that gangster shit that thrilled them. I told them how I went in that door and pulled Lorraine out of that tavern. We sat there for a long while talking. We drank three six-packs. My head felt like a drum as I walked home. Howard walked with me until we reached 70th Street. I was beginning to learn the faces around the neighborhood, and they were beginning to become familiar with my face.

The next day, I called Mr. Crust. I said, "Mr. Crust, I've been so busy that I haven't even called you." "I went on and finished the job." "The bill came to $1700.00." "T tiled the ceiling of the office and the floor, did the plastering in the back, changed the stool, fixed the sink in the bathroom, and put a new door in the bathroom. Hung a new door in the rear of the storefront with a new lock, did all the necessary patch plastering fixed the floor in the rear, and painted the same, $1700.00" "Do you want me to send you a bill in the mail or do you want to come and look at it?" He said, "Today is Monday." "I can get there about 1:00 on Thursday if that's OK with you." I said, "Yes, that is OK with me." He said, "By the way, is your last name Wynn?" I said, "Yes, that's right." He said, "OK, Mr. Wynn, I'll see you on Thursday."

Two or three times, I had let Christine come into the back of my contracting office for drinks, but she was always with someone else, another man. Then she always tried to throw her attention toward me, but I never gave her a play or any intentions that I wanted to play. She was a large woman, about 5'10", weighing about 225 lbs, sloppy looking, and her education was zero. She lived in the apartment building above Stony Liquors. All the side windows of that building faced the Black Marble. She could see anyone who would go in or come out of the Black Marble. It was about 25 steps from her building to the Black Marble on the other side of the street.

On a particular day, I had gone in and bought a ½ pint of Seagram's Gin and a 12-pack of beer. I was on my way back to the office when she called out to me. "Hey, Mr. Wynn," she called out! I turned toward the voice. "If you've got beers in that bag, I sure can use a can because I'm dry today and broke." "Can I come over?" I said, "Yes, come on and I continued walking on to the office." Before long, she had killed the gin and a 6-pack. As she was drinking the last beer of the 6-pack, her eyes started getting that romantic look. She started feeling my arms as I sat across from her in my chair. "Mr. Wynn, you can stop all that wanting to be bashful and acting like you don't know that I like you." She was batting her eyes at me. I said, "You know that I'm married, Christine?" She said, "I don't care, your wife ain't here and what she doesn't know won't hurt her." I said, "Would you care for another beer?" They should be cold in that box by now." She said, "Just one more baby before you come over here in my arms." I stood to go and get the beer out of the box in the back when a knock came to the door. It was Howard, and I could've kissed him. He stepped into the door and said, "Man, I got something good to tell you.,"

Then, he looked over and saw Christine and said, "Hi, Ms. Christine." She dragged a "Hi" out, almost like she was sitting up there, going to sleep. I said, "What's happening, Howard?" He said, "Man, I've been talking to my auntie and she needs a door fixed and she needs a porch fixed and she also has a toilet running over which she needs you to look at right away" Howard said, "She's got money and is ready to pay for the job to be done," and I said, "What we need this time of the afternoon is a car." "Where is the job at, man?" He said, "45th and Chaplain." "Do you know someone who might take us down there?" He said, "No, man, not this time of the day because Mr. Sheet hasn't been in the shop all day."

Then Christine rose out of a nod, and she said, "How much are you paying for a car?" I said, "Do you know someone with a car?" She said, "I know me, I've got a car." I said, "I tell you what, I'll give you $15.00 if you take me down there, and if I get the job, I'll give you $25.00." She said, "OK, but you have to drive." "Do you have a driver's license?" "I told her, "Yes." She took us to her car, which was an old Chrysler parked down the street from her building. She nearly fell into the back seat. Everything that his auntie needed fixing came out to be $580.00. She gave me $225.00 down, and the balance was due upon completion. I gave Christine $25.00 and had Howard help her to her apartment. The next day, I made a deal with Christine to let me rent her car for $15.00 a day. She liked that very much because she knew she could boss me around a little bit with me having her car.

It took Mr. Smith two days to finish the job. It was Thursday, it was time to see Mr. Crust. So, Howard and I sat in the office waiting for him. It was 1:15 when a yellow cab stopped in front of the office, and Mr. Crust got out. He looked up and down the street, then he walked towards the office. Once inside, we shook hands. He looked around the room at the ceiling and floor and the rest of the work, shaking his head in a yes manner. We stopped at the back in the middle of the floor. He said, "You did a nice job with the place." I said, "Thank you!" "This month, July, you won't start paying rent until September." "That will give you a couple of months to get your business going," I said. "Thank you, Mr. Crust!" He said, "Get the jobs, Al, and I'll see you later." I thought that day that Mr. Crust was the only white man who was kin to Jesus Christ.

CHAPTER 12

The week passed quickly as we finished Ms. Corine, Howard's auntie's, job. Mr. Smith was happy with the $160.00 I paid him for the job. That following week I had my phone in, and my windows painted, and I had new curtains hung on the windows and the floors. I had set myself up pretty good now. On weekends, I ran the back of my shop like an after-hours joint. I had bought about ten folding chairs, which were scattered around the room. Calvin had come out and built me a six-stool bar. I bought bar stools from the used furniture store on 68th and Stony Island.

I allowed only Howard in because he was cool, and he acted like he was my bodyguard. Later, I hired Bill, an ex-boxer from 73rd and Dorchester, to be a bouncer on weekends. From time to time, I would see Bullwhip as I went into Black Marble or the Stony Liquors, but most of the time just went into my door. He would put the beg on me. He said, Pimp Daddy, Wynn, how are you doing today, sir.: He would ask with a smile on his face. Some days when he was feeling good, he would tell me how good I looked in the clothes I had on, and then he would come with the drag game. "Come on pimp, let a nigger have a $1.00 or two so I can get me a beer!" I would look at him and say, "Man, how many dollars do you owe me now?" He would d say, "Man, you know that I'm going to pay you as soon as I get a job." I would say, "And you ain't looking too hard, are you?"

He would laugh and say," Man, yes, I am, I'm looking." I would give $2.00 or $3.00 and keep walking. I knew he was pumping me, but I liked the compliments. I needed more than one friend on the streets, and he was a street person. So, I bet him with the $2.00 and $3.00, sometimes I ease $5.00 or $10.00 on him when I had the money. At times, he would say, "Do you need anything, Mr. Wynn?" "Is anybody messing with you?" "If anybody messes with you let me know, I've got you." "Call on me, man," he would say as he walked away.

I was getting around every day now and doing little jobs, screen doors, windows, door locks, and rodding out toilets. Some days, I would be late getting back from 47th Street or wherever I had gone, and Christine would come to my shop and raise hell like I had a Lincoln Continental or something. Howard said, Man, why are you putting up with that old drunken woman's conversations" "I would get me a truck or something, man, I wouldn't be putting up with that bullshit." I said, "I just let her talk, Howard, it don't mean shit."

It had been about two months since the place opened, and we sat around the two desks that I had. One desk, which was the larger desk, sat in front of the middle window. That was my desk. The smaller desk sat about three or four steps from the front door. Just enough room for a person to stop at another receptionist's desk and close the door. A chair sat on the side of that desk, and a chair sat on the side of my desk. Howard sat at the receptionist's desk with his feet on it. We were drinking beer in glasses from a quart that we had when the telephone rang. I answered it. "Hello, I said, "Al Wynn's Contracting." The voice said, "Hi, Al, how's business?" I said, "Oh, Mr. Crust, how are you?" "I'm not doing too badly." I told him, "I'm just doing small jobs, no big jobs yet." He told me, "Well, I want you to look at a job for me." I replied, "Yes, sir, yes, sir!"

I looked over at Howard and blinked my eye. He took his feet off the desk and walked over toward me. "I want you to look at those garages in the back of the building." "I think there are six individual garages." "I want you to look at those doors and see what we can do for them." "I want you to look at the roof of the garages." "Then, in the back of the six storefronts, there are holes in the bricks that need tuckpointing." "There are six storefronts where you are, I need you to scrape down those bars on the windows because they're all rusting." "Take your time and give me a price on that and I want you to mail it to me. It would be good if you could get it in here before Thursday because we have board meetings on Thursdays."

That damn Fire Department on 69th and Dante right down the street from you is giving me hell about this job." "So, get on it right away." "Don't do any work until I give you my approval." "Do you understand that?" I said, "Yes sir." He said, "OK, kid, see you later." I jumped up and said, "Here it is, Howard, this is some money!" He said, "What is it?" I said, "This whole goddamn building we must remodel it!"

Howard and I spent about two or three hours getting measurements and looking at the chipped paint on the garage and bricks and the caked-up rust that was on the window bars. There were another two hours spent writing it up. Since I had no secretary, I had to go to the secretarial service on 47th and Michigan. I couldn't go to Mr. Thomas, my man, because they had him in jail. The secretary on 447th and Michigan is very good at her typing. Within an hour, she had drawn up a contract. I didn't want to stick the man up or scare him half to death, so I made up a contract for $1900.00, and I put it into an envelope and mailed it to him that night. It was Tuesday night so he should get it at least by Thursday.

That evening, I stopped by 47th and the L station and told Harvey, Calvin, and Paul about the call I had gotten from my landlord. Calvin promised me that he would bring Harvey out to the office the next day to look at the rusty bars and the painting. Calvin would take care of the carpentry work, the tuckpointing, and the roofing. I asked Calvin to have Mr. Smith help him with whatever he needed to do, and Howard, too. He agreed to it.

CHAPTER 13

After Calvin got through looking at both roofs, the carpentry work, and the tuck pointing we sat in my office with him, Bily, Harvey, Howard, and me drinking beer. I bought a case of Budweiser that sat on the desk in my office. Howard was taking the rest of the beers and putting them in the refrigerator while Billy and Harvey were listening to Calvin as he was speaking to me. "How much did you say you charged the man, Al?" I said, "$1900.00, I didn't want to scare him, and I needed the job." He said, "I can understand that, but the job is worth about $10,000.00. "The money that you're charging him is just enough for the materials." "If you can, you'd better change your price right away because you're going into the hole with this job."

I didn't call Mr. Crust that Thursday. I was going to call him that Friday at about 1:00, but to my surprise, the telephone rang at about 9:30 that Friday morning, and I answered it. Mr. Crust was on the other end. He hollered out, "Al, what the hell is this!" My stomach started knotting up, I thought I had overcharged him. I said, "If it's too much, I can change it." He said, "Hell, too much, it's not enough, people will think that you don't know what you're doing." "Send me a contract that makes some sense, a Contract that

I can live with!" "Well, Mr. Crust, while you're here on the phone can you live with a contract that's $7500.0?" He said, "Now, that makes better sense, send me that and itemize it." I did, I sent him the contract, and in a week, I had a $3500.00 check in my hand from him.

The ball started rolling. Calvin and Mr. Smith worked together on the tuckpointing and the roof. Howard did the scraping for Harvey. Harvey did all the painting. Some of the guys of Howard's age came around to look at the work that was being done. They would stand around and drink their wine, whiskey, or beer and signify with Howard until they got tired and wandered away.

I was busy running from one side of the building to the other taking care of business, I didn't have time for my phone. So, I hired a little hoe girl that they called Sug to do my secretarial work, like taking notes and answering the phone. Etc. All the men loved Sug. She was petite, wore nice clothes, and had the gift of gab. She kept the office spotless, and she did my running to the store for me. She reminded me of my important calls. She seemed to have had my back with the business and the welfare of the office.

She was very reliable and punctual. So, I left all the office work in her hands. I was still using Christine's car. I was almost keeping the car now in the daytime and most of the night. After getting the job, I started paying Christine $40.00 a day and keeping her supplied with beer. She was so drunk sometimes that she didn't know whether I had paid her or not. A week and a half had passed, and we were getting around to putting the finishing touches on the job. Doing the window bars and the rear doors of the storefronts.

On a particular day, I went to the 67th Street Fish House to get my men some lunch. As I entered the door, I saw Eddie standing in line ordering some fish. He looked up and we saw each other at the same time, he smiled and said, "My man, Al!" I said, "What's happening, Eddie, I heard that you were home." He said, "Yeah, man." After we had ordered our fish and were standing outside by the ragged Chrysler, he said, "Man, it's about time you get another car." I said, "Man, this ain't my car, this is a friend of mine's car." "Man, it looks tired." I said, "What are you doing out here, man?" "Where are you at now?" He said, "I'm right down the street at the Southmoore." I work for Jet." "I drive a Livery cab."

I said, "Well, man, I've got a place down the street at 6916 Stony Island." "It's an after-hours joint." "Why don't you come down there and visit me and bring your girl or just come down there with some friends, man, and have a drink with me?" He said, "Where did you say that is again? I might come down tonight." I said, "Come on down there you know that you don't need any money to come there, you're my main man." "The address is 6916 Stony Island, just ring the front bell to the storefront." He said, "Yeah, man, I might drop in on you tonight." "What time do you leave?" I said, "I usually be around there until about 10:00, I don't have anything else to do." He said, "Yeah, OK, I might be around there about 8:00," I said, "Cool man, cool." "I need someone like you to hang out for a minute." I went to the shop, the guys were working very hard that day, trying to finish up for Friday, and it was Wednesday.

Everybody had left except Howard, and we sat in the front office with the lights out looking out the front window, then I saw Eddie's cab roll up in front of my shop. He had a young lady with him. As they came into the office and walked to the bar, I noticed her for the first time. She looked to be about 40 years old and on the heavy side, with big buttocks and hips. Her name was Eva. Eddie introduced her to me. I, in turn, introduced Howard to the two of them. I had two couches and three loveseats in a circle. I sat on one of the love seats. Howard sat in another one and Eddie and the young lady sat on the couch. We were having lots of fun drinking and laughing.

Eddie was telling jokes about me and that coal man's coat that I used to wear. "That damn coat swallowed him," Eddie said as he laughed out. "He looked like a damn dwarf in it." "Al used to get the money, though." "Al could get that money from them, women."

I said, "I tried, didn't I?" He said, "You got the money!" "I was there with you!" Eva looked at Eddie as he was laughing about the coat and said, "Since you think Al is so good at getting money from women, why don't you let him collect that $50.00 from that woman that owes you $50.00 at the cab stand?" Eddie damn near high sipped of the whiskey in his glass and brought it back down and said, "Now, that's a damn good idea!" Eva asked Eddie, "Why don't we introduce Al to Ms. Carrie, with her rich ass?" I asked, "Who is Ms. Carrie?" Eddie replied, "Some rich broad sown there who hit my car." "I rent my cab, she owns about two or three cars, and she rents her cars out to Jet Livery. "She drives her brand-new car." "She's also a supervisor down at the aid office on 21st and Michigan." "She had her car parked in front of mine." "I know that the old hag can't drive." "She tried to get her car out of a hole, and she hit mine." "She's a nice lady and I don't want to slap the piss out of her, so I said just let it pass."

"Now I'm going to do this for you," Mr. Eddie Eva said while lifting her glass into the air as if she were giving a toast. "If Al here can get your $50.00 in any kind of way from her as cheap as she is, then I'm going to give you $100.00." Eddie said, "I'll take that bet. How long does he have to get it? How long will you give him to get it?" She said, "Knowing how cheap that woman is what do you need a year?" Eddie said, "Let's be serious, I trust my little buddy here." "He won't need a year; will a month be fair?" "If we've got a bet and if you win, I'll pay you. But if I win, will you pay me the hundred dollars if he gets the $50.00 out of her and doesn't have to pay her back within a month?" Eva said, "That's fair enough."

Eddie asked, "How are we going to introduce him to her?" Eva replied, "That's the thing." I said, "I have an idea." They said, "What is it?" I said, "Which one of all is the closest to her?" Eddie said, "Eva is, they're partners." Eva is the dispatcher, and she throws out Carrie's extra jobs. In return for the jobs, Carrie throws her out so they're close." I replied, "Well, if you want to Eva, you can tell Carrie that you have a cousin from out of town, Georgia, or Alabama. Who wants to work, and he wants to learn the city and you think that she would be the best person to teach him." "You can tell her that you would appreciate it if she could teach him to drive and tell her that it would be a personal favor to you if she could do that." Eva understood what she had to do.

The weeks passed and I finished the job for Mr. Crust. I had paid my men and paid all my debts, and I gave my wife some money and I had about $700.00 left in my pocket to play with. I went gambling and lost about $300.00 of those dollars. I didn't want to get broke, so I left the game, that wasn't my night. The next morning, I sat at my desk across from Sug and Howard. Howard was sitting in the chair beside Sug's desk. There weren't any more jobs and we were waiting there like vultures for the telephone to ring and it did. It was Eva. "Hi, cuz," she said. I said, "Hi Eva." She said, "I have Ms. Carrie on the other line." "She wants very much to meet you and if you still want to learn the city you can start tonight at 6:00 and she'll meet you at the cab stand."

I met Ms. Carrie at about 6:15 at the cab stand. Only two or three men stood on the outside of the door at the cab stand while Eva and Ms. Carrie sat inside the cab stand. Eva saw me and she took off the headphones and turned off the microphone and she introduced us. Ms. Carrie stood, and I damn near undressed her with one look. She seemed to be about 5'6" tall, with a small waist and big hips. She wore boots to her knees with her pants tucked in them. She had mingled gray hair that kind of curled up in a fluff roll over her forehead. She wasn't pretty, but she was very attractive. I could see the twinkle in her eyes too as she stared into mine. Eva went on talking.

"Ms. Carrie thinks that the best way for you to learn the city is by driving for her." I said, "Whatever you all say." Eva said, "OK, cuz, you're on your own." "Yeah, take care of my cousin, Carrie." She said, "Yeah, OK," as we walked out the rear door to her car. She gave me the key to her car. I unlocked her door and held the door open for her to get in then I walked around to the driver's side and got under the wheel It was a black Fairlane Ford. You couldn't hear the motor when I cranked it up, it sounded so smooth. Before I could ask Carrie where we were going, Eva's voice came over the radio. "OK, Carrie buckle up, I have a fare at 4515 Champlain." "I told the customer that you would be there in 30 minutes." Ms. Carrie picked up the microphone and said "10/4." I kind of smiled to myself because 4515 Champlain was right down the street from where I lived with my mother at 417 E. 45th Street.

Carrie said, "OK, Al, there are three ways that we can get there." "Come out of the alley and make a left and to Stony Island." "The next block is Stony, make a left and we're going to 60th and Stony, which is the mid-way." I wanted so badly to tell her that she would catch all those lights going that way. It would be better to go through the park and come out at 4th Street, but I held my thoughts and went her way to the Mid-Way. She was so busy talking and looking at me that she didn't know when we got to the Mid-Way. I asked her, "Is this where you're talking about, 60th Street?" She said, "Yes, turn here." She said, "Go on this street until you get to Cottage Grove and turn right." I damn nearly got us into the address, but I followed her directions and obeyed every stop sign and light to impress her by driving very carefully.

We picked up a passenger who wanted to go downtown to the Greyhound Bus Station. I followed her directions to get there. Don't get me wrong, Ms. Carrie was an intelligent conservative woman and a supervisor at the Aid Office, but for the next three days, Ms. Carrie had gotten her hair done and was damn near wearing a Minnie skirt sitting up there next to me. Three or four cab drivers were walking in and out of the cab stand. Only me, Eva, Eddie, and Ms. Carrie were in the dispatch room. Ms. Carrie made an excuse to go to the bathroom. Eddie and Eva started looking at me and laughing. I said, "What's wrong, what's the matter?" Eva looked at Eddie and then at me and said, "You've got her, brother." "Carrie doesn't wear a dress unless she's going to church." "Now, she's wear-ing those Minnie skirts." "She wants to show off those big thighs to you. "Those knees and legs, too," Eddie said. "I bet if you say hotel, she will say yes." I looked at Edie and smiled, Ms. Carrie was back now, and we left for our first trip. I said, "Carrie, you know I like you, don't you?" She said, "Yeah, I believe you like me." I said, "Well, I don't want to hurt you." She said, "What are you talking about?" I said, "You're going to have to put those pants back on because if I keep looking at those big pretty legs of yours, I'm going to have a wreck." She started laughing. She said, "Are you serious?" I said, "I'm dead serious, so, if you don't want me getting out of place with you or out of hand, you wear those pants tomorrow."

"So, if you come to work wearing anything but those pants, we're not going to work tomorrow." "We are going to be somewhere having a serious talk."

The next day, hoping for the best of the situation between Ms. Carrie and me, I brushed my teeth well, put on my best cologne and a clean shirt, and brushed my hair. I usually meet Carrie at the cab-stand at 6:00, but I was there early on this day at 5:00 to see Eddie and Eva. To my surprise, Carrie was there at 5:30 wearing a blue skirt that looked shorter than the first one she wore. She came in smiling and speaking to Eva and Eddie. She looked over at me and spoke. "How are you feeling today, Mr. Wynn? I said, "I'm feeling good." She said, "Come on, tonight I'm driving." She drove the car down to 71st and Stony Island ad turned left and went to South Shore Drove. It wasn't a surprise to me when she parked in the lot of the Motel on 79th and South Shore Drive. She then told me "Well, Mr. Wynn, you wait right here until I get the key."

We were inside the room now and I took my time caressing her. First, I squeezed her breast real softly, then rubbed her shoulders, her side, and then hie thighs. I kissed her softly on her neck. Occasionally, dragging my tongue down her breast to the tip of her nipples, then kiss her softly on her stomach, then her thighs, her neck, and her ears. My hands fell between her legs, and I rubbed the inside of her thighs very softly. Her breathing became louder as she whispered in my ear, "Come on baby, I'm ready for you." I ignored her as my tongue darted from side to side on her neck and ear. I bit her ear lobes softly as my tongue reached back to her nipple. "Please, baby," she whispered, softly, fuck me!!" I then eased into her very gently.

After we made love, I washed up, and I was putting on my shoes as Carrie came out of the bathroom, mumbling to herself and making up the bed. "You know that fucked up!" "You fucked up now!!" I said, "Carrie, you don't have to make the bed." She said, "You then fucked up now!" I said, "How have I fucked up?" She said, "You then stirred in the sugar bowl." Then she said, "She hadn't had anybody like me in years. When we left the motel, it had started to rain. She took me back to the old Chrysler that I had parked to the curb about two or three doors from the cabstand. We hadn't said anything to each other on the way back to the car. When we got to the car, we each said "goodnight." I got out and she drove away.

CHAPTER 14

I kept getting small jobs while I worked during the day and drove for Carrie at night. When we would get together, she showered me with thousands of questions. She wanted to know where my mother lived, how many brothers and sisters I had, and if I had ever been married. I swallowed hard and turned the car left on 35th Street heading to Michigan Avenue. I looked out the window and lied, "No," I said, "I've never been married." "I haven't found the right lady yet." I smiled and looked at her.

She didn't say another word as she sat quietly as we picked up the passenger on 36th Street. He tipped me a couple of dollars and got out of the cab. She said, "Baby, I don't feel like working all night let's stop here and have a drink." I didn't want to go to the Brown Derby because I knew the owner and the bartender, Leo, but I had to play my hand with Carrie as the naïve young man from down south. So, I hurried up through the lounge, knowing where the back tables were as she followed and seated herself in one of the booths I said, "Do you want me to order for you, baby?" She said, "Order me a pink lady and get what you want."

I made my way through the crowd to the front of the bar. It was a round bar shaped like an "O," with about 27-30 stools around it.

The drinks sat in the middle of the bar. I made my way to the front of the bar out of Carrie's view. Leo was around on the other side of the bar, and I made my way to him, and he recognized me. "Al, when did you come in?" "I didn't see you come in!" I said, "Just a while ago, but listen, Leo." "I'm with a nice young lady over there in the corner who thinks that I'm right out of the Bayou." "So, you don't know me, OK?" He said, "I got you."

I ordered the drinks, and before long, the girl was at our booth serving us. Carrie had a curly roll on the top of her hair. After about two or three drinks, the roll had dropped to her shoulders. Her eyes had a glassy look now as he stared into my eyes. She said, "Al, I kind of like you, and I'm getting damn tired of staying by myself." "I'm not a rich lady." "I own my house and three cabs, and you know, of course, I work for the Public Aid Office. "I've been knowing you, baby, for about three or four weeks now." "I have made u my mind that you are the one that I want to see lying next to me at night in my bed."

"I will not allow myself to just live with a man." "I want you to know that I go to church every Sunday, and I want to keep everything upfront with you." "I have a ten-year-old granddaughter." My daughter and her husband have finished college, and they both have good jobs." "My daughter is in no way a burden to me at all." "I'm telling you this because everything that I own is willed to my daughter, and she knows this." "If I get married, then whatever I accumulate with my husband will be his if something happens to me." "I feel good about us, and I feel that we could accumulate a whole lot together." Eva and Eddie had told me about your little after-hours joint, which you never invited me to, and I know you're a contractor." "I also know about that little lady that you are borrowing a car from, and you have to rush away from me when we're together to take it back to her." "Is she your woman? Who is she to you?

I replied," She's just some woman who wishes she could just get a moment of my time, but all I'm interested in is that car." "I need a ride bad!" "If I had a car, I would push her away from me so fast that her head would spin around." I looked away from her, sipping on my drink and mumbling out loud to myself. "I just need a break." "What do you need, Al?" she asked while leaning back in the booth and looking at me inquisitively?" I then asked her, "Do you want to know what I need, Carrie?" She said, "Yes, tell me." I told her, "I need a stake to get on my feet with my contracting, but what I need is a car, and mostly, darling, I need you." "Then I can show you how much money I can make." "I used to do all of those things down south, but I had little trouble and had to come here." "Nothing really bad, just a falling out with a family member." "Then I could get rid of that pest."

She told me, I'm not proposing to you, Al, but I want to ask you how you would feel about settling down with me if there's no one else in your life and you're serious about me?" "If you mean this, Carrie, I feel like I'm the luckiest person in the world to meet someone like you." She said, "Well, if this is the case, Al, I have some vacation time coming next month." Can we make a date for that Sunday on the 15th," and can we get married in my church after the service? "If you need some time to think about it, then let me know now." I said, "I'd be a damn fool to wait another day." "Yes, darling, it can happen on the 15th." She said, "OK, let's get another drink, and you can go home with me tonight and eat some supper." "You're going to eat some of my cooking tonight, Mr. Wynn." I said, "Why not?"

Carrie excused herself to go to the bathroom. I called Nella and told her that I would be out gambling all night. Carrie lay back on the passenger side with her eyes closed after telling me the location of her house at 76th and Wentworth. While I was driving her home, she said, "Al, I know I'm older than you are, are you sure this is what you want?" "I'm sure, baby, I wouldn't have said it if I didn't mean it." "Only money gets old, baby," I told her as I looked at her. "If you were any younger, I couldn't have kept up with you the other night." "You are as mellow as a peach, darling, and don't you ever forget it." After that, there was silence.

CHAPTER 15

It was an exciting evening with Carrie. I enjoyed her company. Candlelight, steaks, and sex set the mood for the evening. The next morning, bright and early, around 6:00, Carrie awakened with a towel and said, "Breakfast will be ready shortly!" After the shower, we sat across from each other, eating breakfast. To the right of us were two sliding glass doors that gave a picturesque view of an enclosed fence around a huge backyard. Roses and Lilies surrounded the patio in front of the range in her yard. Her garage roof was wide, covering some parts of the patio, and the roof had rod iron posts on each side of the patio. A barbeque grill sat on the patio in the corner. I turned back to my bacon and eggs and when I looked up from my plate, she was looking at me, smiling. I said, "It's a lovely view." She said, "Yes, it is lovely."

It was 8:20 when she dropped me off in front of my office. I kissed her softly on the lips as I got out of the car and wished her a pleasant day at work. As I unlocked my door to the office, I thought about Nella and the kids. I thought about how sweet it would be if I weren't married, with an opportunity like marrying Carrie available to me now. She had backed me into a corner with that marriage stuff, but that was a month away, so I'll worry about that closer to the date. My thing now was to pressure her into getting the car. I had to pressure her in such a way for her to realize that either she could buy this car now or we wouldn't be getting married, and she would lose me.

I walked through the office, opened the door that separated the office from the rear, went into the refrigerator, removed a cold Budweiser from the refrigerator, and walked back to my desk. I had finished sipping my beer at about a quarter till 10:00. The sun was shining brightly through the curtains, and my thoughts were interrupted by a loud knock on the door. I got up and peeped out of the blinds on the door. It was Howard, and right after seeing the beer bottle on the desk, he asked, "Do you have another beer, man, I could use one because I've got a hell of a headache?" I said, "Yeah, man, and bring me one back, too." He said, "Where's Sug at? isn't she supposed to be here at 9:00?" I said, "I don't remember, man, she asked to be off to take her grandmother to the dentist." He said, "Oh, yeah, man, that's right, you told her to come in tomorrow." "You have to forgive me, Al, man, I put one on last night and my head is still busting," he said while stumbling over to Sug's seat at her desk.

I told him, "Drink that beer, man, you'll be alright in a few minutes." "If not, we'll get a shot when you get some food in our stomach." He took a big swallow of the beer and let the bottle come back down to the desk with a slight bang. "What did you do, Mr. Wynn, last night?" "Well, I had an exciting afternoon, so exciting that I ended up getting engaged to be married." He asked, "How in the hell did you do that when you're already married?" I replied, "That's why it is so exciting. I wonder how in the hell I did that." He said, "With whom, the cab driver?" I said, "Yeah!" I said, "She asked me what I want in life?" I told her, "I wanted a car and some other things." You see, Howard, a person has to learn from the past."

"I know another lady who asked me what I wanted years ago, her name was Bertha Hill." "I want to use what I learned from the experience with her to lay on Carrie." Howard asked, "Oh, what are you going to lay on her?" I responded, "Sweet talk, beef, and bull." Howard asked me, "What the hell is that?" I replied, "Man, I'm going to sweet talk her, you know what that is, and I'm going to lay this good beef on her, and you know what that is, I'm talking about sex, and I'm going to bullshit her so much that she is going to need napkins,' Howard gave out a big loud laugh and said, "Man, you're full of shit." I said, "That's what I'm trying to tell you, Howard."

We talked and laughed and drank beers until noon, and then the telephone rang. It was Christine. She wanted to know if I needed the car for today because she could use that $15.00, and she needed a drink, and she could come over. I told her yes. I had sent Howard for a fresh six-pack when the telephone rang again. I answered, "Al Wynn's Contracting." She said, "Hello, darling, how are you feeling today? I said, "Carrie." She said, "Yeah, who did you think it was, one of your other ladies?" I said, "I don't have any ladies except you, baby." "Last night, I should have told you that I showed you with my heart and mind." She said, "I've been thinking about you, darling, and I hope that you're not just bullshitting me and that you are really real in what you're saying." She said, "You know what you said last night bout the marriage and I want to make sure that you want this and if you need any more time, I wish you would let me know." "If you are sure, I'm going to call my pastor and make the arrangements for the 15th." I said, "I wasn't drunk when I said it, and if I said it, I meant it." "I'm ready for you, baby." She said, "I'm so happy that you said that, and I tell you what you do today, you go and get that lady's little funny-looking car and go and try to see if you can find what you want."

She told me, "Tomorrow, when I'm off work at 2:00, we'll go and check it out, is that satisfactory to you, Mr. Wynn?" I told her, "Oh, baby, you make me so happy that I want to plant 1,000 kisses on you from your toes to your ear lobes. Thank you!" "I'll see you later, Mr. Wynn, she said and hung up as Howard was entering the door. I said, "I've got it, Howard!!' He asked, "Got what?" I replied, "She just called and told me to go and pick out my car." He said, "Man, you're bullshitting!!!" I said, "No, I ain't bullshitting you, man, we just got through talking about that." He said, "Man, no shit, for real?"

Before Christine left, I gave her two beers and $15.00 and I got the keys to her car. Fifteen minutes later we were sitting at the car dealership at 71st and Stony Island, across the street from the Three Sisters Restaurant. Before I could get into the lot, I saw the car of my desire. It was a money-green Coupe De Ville Cadillac with thin white wall tires, a black interior, and a black vinyl top. I opened the door to the driver's seat, and the big, tall black seat sat up tall. I sat under the wheel. Howard came up to the car and said, "Man, it's just like heaven in here, isn't it?" I replied, Yeah, it is, man." He asked, "Do you think she'll buy you this?" I told him, "We won't know until we see, right, Howard?"

By this time, the salesman was coming towards us. I got out of the car. He said, "It's a honey, isn't it?" I replied, "It sure is." I asked him, "What year is this?" He replied, "It's a 1966 Coupe Deville Brohan. Would you like to go to the office and talk about it? I said, "Yes, I would." We must have talked and negotiated in there for about an hour, with him talking and checking prices. The final analysis was that he could let me have the car for $2,000.00 down and a note. The salesman said, "How's your credit?" I said, "Good." I told him I owned a house and that was it." After checking, he told me that I could have the car, but I would need a cosigner. I asked him if

I could bring the cosigner in the next day because she was at work, and he agreed. I told him about 3.00 the next day. Howard and I left the lot happy, and we were going to get drunk with Mr. Sheet to celebrate my good fortune.

CHAPTER 16

I waited impatiently with Howard the next day for Carrie. Finally, at about 3:15, the horn blew outside. It was Carrie, although I had talked to her about fifteen times already that day, explaining that I had found the car of my dreams and how happy I was to see it. I never told her about the phone, the make, or the model of the car. I explained to her that I needed a co-signer and what the down payment and the notes would be. I was afraid that her impression of me getting a Cadillac would be that I wanted to play other than work, not buy a truck or a station wagon. As we rode the car lot, I said, "Carrie, the reason that I'm getting a car is first, because I want to get jobs from real estate and insurance companies, etc." "Their first impression will be a lasting one." "Therefore, I want their first impression to be the right one." "So, with a couple of jobs, I can get that station wagon or a truck to haul my materials around in." "I just wanted you to know the reason why I'm getting a car first." It relieved my mind as she answered me, "It's your show, baby, I just want to be a part of it." "I sweetened the cake more by saying, "You're going to play a greater part next month on the 15th."

She smiled as she pulled up on the car lot. We were greeted by the salesman I had talked to the day before. He asked, "Is the co-signer you were talking about, AL?" I said, "Yes." He pulled back her chair for her in front of his desk. She was seated and I sat in the chair next to her. "Let me get your file, the salesman said as he reached into the bottom drawer of his desk. He pulled out a manilla envelope that read, "Al Wynn" on the front of it. He opened it up and asked Carrie, "Did he tell you what the car notes and the price of the war would be?" "Yes, he did "Carrie replied. The salesman said, with a down payment of $200.00, the notes are going to be $193.00 including insurance for 36 months."

The salesman told Carrie that the total price of the car was $8,948.00, and he went on to say, "Again, before you sign, you are being co-signer, you will be responsible for the notes, do you understand that?" She said, "Yes." He said, "OK, then go ahead and sign and date the papers." After that, Carrie reached into her purse, took a rubber band off a stack of $100.00 bills, and gave him the $2,000.00. She then placed the rubber band back around the money and stuck it back into her purse. He counted the money, then made a call and asked, "Is, Mr. Wynn's car washed?" He hung up the phone and counted the money again. He took the money to the cashier and returned with a receipt placed the receipt in an envelope along with the papers for the car and handed the envelope to me. I pointed to Carrie, and he handed it to her.

Before long, they had brought the car in front of the door. "My, that's beautiful, is that your car?" I said, "Yes, that's my car." He provided two sets of keys. He asked me, "Would you like for her to have a set of keys?" I was between the devil and the deep blue sea, so I said, "Of course, give her a set." She said, "Darling, would you like to go and have dinner? Then we could go to the Thunderbird, or we could go to my house." I said, "What would you like to do?" She said, "Since you have your big, beautiful car, I figured that we could go out to dinner, and then we could go to the Thunderbird." "You can take me home and let me park my car, and then we could go to dinner." She left the Cadillac and headed over to her car in the car lot. I followed her to 76th and Lafayette, where she pulled into her garage. I waited, and after a while, she came through her side gate and climbed into Bromham. I asked her, "Would you like to drive?" She said, "No, baby, I'm tired of driving, and I'm just relaxing." "You drive."

She then asked me, "Why don't we have dinner at Mabelle's on 51st Street?" She looked over at me and started telling me where Maybelle's is on 51st Street and the name "H&H." She thought she was telling me something I didn't know, and I followed her directions to H&H. It was an exciting evening at the motel; the night slipped away with drinks and laughter. The morning brought on another surprise. I washed up and dressed at the motel. Carrie told me that she had taken the day off because she had to take care of some business with her cab license, so she had to go downtown. She sat in a chair near the bed and told me to sit down.

She said, "Al, I'm taking a hell of a chance with you." "Some guys take advantage of situations like we have, but I hope you're not one of those guys." "So, I got $7,000.00 out of the bank, you said the other night that you need a break, and this is your break from me." "I'm trying to help you to make your dreams come true." "So, you've got the car and I'm fixing to give you this $5,000.00." "You can get your truck out of it, or you can get your station wagon, whatever." "Maybe you can open yourself up a little bank account, it's up to you to do whatever you want to do with the money," "I figure it's a good stake for you to get started, and it is an investment for the future for both of us." "So, you can get me back to my car because I don't have time to have breakfast with you." "I have to go and take care of my business, and you can go and take care of yours," and as we stood, she came over to me and whispered in my ear and said, "I love you, baby," and we left in my dream car.

CHAPTER 17

headed for home right away because I had told Nella the lie about being out gambling all night and I wanted to please her by showing her the substantial evidence of my winnings. Like I always did when I won money gambling, I threw it all on the bed and let her play with it and she had fun doing so After giving her about $300.00 for herself, I told her my plans to buy a car and that I was leaving to go and get my hair done and go shopping for myself. I asked her, "Is that OK?" She said, "Sure, baby, but you don't ever stay home, you're always on the run." I said, "Just run this over to the closet or whatever it is you put my money," I had given Nella $300.00 for herself which left me with $4700.00. So, I took $1700.00 with me and gave her the $3,999.00 to put up for me and I left.

My stop was the House of Nelson on Cottage Grove near the Mansfield Hotel on 64th and Cottage Grove. I had a haircut and finger waves. The weather was turning cool because it was going into the fall of the year. I headed for 47th Street. I stopped in Max's clothing Store and bought about five sweaters at $60.00 a piece, about five pairs of slacks to match the sweaters, and two or three belts. Then, I went into Albert's Hat Shop; and bought a cowboy-style Stetson hat that had a rolled long brim. The hat made you look like a gangster or a big-time player. At Albert's, I also bought about five or six pairs of socks. The only thing I knew was missing now was a couple of lightweight jackets.

I had promised myself a leather jacket, so, I went to the Leather House on 87th Street near Jeffrey. I bought a short tan leather jacket for about $150.00. I kept looking around the store for black leather. The ones that I saw were either too long or too short. I wanted black leather to match the Dobbs hat. I asked the salesman, "Are these the only black leather jackets that you have? He said, "These are the only ones that I have, but how much money did you want to spend on a jacket?" I said, "Why do you ask that? Aren't the prices about the same?" "I asked you because I have one heart that was made up for an actor." "He put the necessary money down to have it made, but his balance is $750.00, and the owner is willing to let it go for $350.00" "Would you like to see it?" "It's in the back of the store." I said, "Yes, yes I would like to see it."

He brought it out in a bag and hung it on a hanger right in front of the counter. I fell in love with it as soon as I saw it. It was a thin-looking jacket that seemed like a person could wring out the water in it with bare hands. It had a strip of cowhide, black, brown, and white, coming from the back of the jacket over the right-hand shoulder. It was a beautiful jacket. It was hip-length, and it had buttons instead of a zipper. I said, "You made my day, my man, let me try it on," It was a perfect fit. I wore my average clothes throughout the day, but everybody in the neighborhood admired my beautiful Coup DeVille. It was the second day of having the car when Sug, Howard, and I sat in the office discussing my play with Carrie. Sug said, "That woman must love you; that's a beautiful car."

I was so busy handling business that I hadn't seen Christine in a couple of days. The telephone rang, and Sug answered the phone. "Al Wynn's Contracting," Sug said in a loud voice. "Oh, yes, darling, he's here," and Sug handed me the phone. She made a motion with her mouth, "It's Christine." "Hi, Al," Christine said on the phone. I said, "Hello, Christine, what's going on?" She said, "I haven't seen you in a couple of days, you didn't need the car?" I said, "No, I've been taking care of some business." "You've been taking care of business without a car; I can't understand that." "You know that I'm broke, and I need a drink." I told her, "I don't need the car, Christine, but you can come over and I'll buy you a drink." Howard said, "Man, I want to see this shit because I've been praying for the day that you get a car." "Mabe now that you've got your car she'll keep her drunk ass at home."

Before long, Christine walked through the door. I had Howard bring out a six-pack, and we were all drinking that day inside the office. I gave Christine my seat, and I sat partially on my desk. Howard stood by the door, looking out. I said, "Christine, we're drinking gin, would you like some, and you can have a beer?" She said, "Oh yeah, I would appreciate that." After a couple of shots, Christine started talking wildly. She said, "I need some money to pay my telephone bill." "I need about $45.00, and you can keep the car for three days, OK, Al?" I told her, "I don't need that car, Christine," I told her that. Howard burst out and said, "Christine, you didn't know Al has a car?" "Everybody knows Al has a car except you." She said, "No, I didn't know he had a car, where is it?" Howard opened the front door wide and said, "There it is!"

The green Bromham was parked at the curb in front of the door. Christine nearly dropped her glass. She said, "You are lying, where did he get a car like that?" Sug looked at her ad and said, "That's Al's car, Christine, and it's pretty, isn't it? She said, "Really pretty." She went back to her seat with her head kind of drooping. I said, "Christine, you and I are still OK, I appreciate very much you letting me use your car." "Christine, I'm going to let you have the

$45.00 for your telephone bill. you just let me know when you're going to pay it back." "The only time that I can pay it back is the 1st of the month." I flashed my bankroll and peeled off $45.00 from the bottom of the stack. We had a couple more drinks together, and then I locked up my office and got ready to meet Carrie at the cab stand.

I arrived there about an hour before Carrie was supposed to be there. I showed the car to Eddie and Eva. Eddie looked at Eva and said, "What did I tell you, what did I tell you, pay me my money." Eva said, "Wait a minute, man, I'm going to pay you your damn money, but you are going to have to wait till I get paid or let me pay you in installments because he did it too damn fast for me." A $10,000 car, shit, that's fast!"

I had parked the car right in front of the cab stand, and Eva had left her office to see the car. Other drivers were out in front, and they just looked at the car and looked at us; they had no idea what the conversation was about. We stepped back into the office. I said, "Wait just a minute, I don't want any fighting over any money!' They just looked at me, especially Eva, she seemed shocked that she had to pay that $10.00 back. I reached into my pocket and skimmed that same bankroll back. "I'm going to pay that $100.00 for you, Eva." She said, "Really!!"

I told Eva, "You know Al loves you, and I'm going to give Eddie and you $100.00, and I skinned the bankroll back and gave each of them $100.00. I told them, "I appreciate what both of you did for me by introducing me to Carrie Reid." Eva said, "Al, I must say this, and I hope you forgive me for saying it." She said, "I agree with Eddie, you are a "motherfucker!!!" Eddie said, "I tried to tell you that, but you wouldn't believe me, you had to see it for yourself."

We laughed and joked for about an hour while Eva was taking calls and directing cabs to their destination. Eva was telling Eddie and me about her playing the organ in her church when Carrie walked into the office. I looked up at Carrie and said, "You are kind of late, aren't you?" She said, "Yes, I had to make a stop." "Have you been here long?" I said, "About an hour, but I wanted to see Eddie, anyway." She said, "Well, are you ready to get started?" I said, "Yes, do you want me to park my car in the lot, the parking lot that was across the street from the South Moor Hotel." She said, "Yes, I'll come over and get you." Right away, Eva called with a fare. It was at 87th and Pauline. Tonight, Carrie drove, and I sat there in the front seat just relaxing.

CHAPTER 18

It wasn't too long before it was September 15th, and wedding bells were in the air. She could hardly wait for that day, and now it was here. That Sunday at about 5:00 pm, we stepped up to the altar in front of the preacher. We had about three of her friends as witnesses. I slid the ring on her finger, and not long after, the preacher said, "I now pronounce you man and wife." "You may kiss the bride." We went out to dinner at H&H Restaurant on 51st and Indiana, and then to the Brown Derby where we drank, laughed, and talked until about midnight. When we were on our way to my new home at 76 & Lafayette.

She had a nice breakfast fixed that morning at about 100.00 when she awakened me. "Come on, get up, darling. Your breakfast is ready, and I have clean towels in the bathroom you can take a shower and then you can get dressed and come and eat." She bent over and kissed me on my forehead and then she left the room. She said, "You make my 5th husband." I said, "Your 5th husband?" She said, "Yes." "Didn't I tell you that I had been married four times?" I said, "No!" "Where are all of them living now?" I asked her, placing the bone back into my mouth, I was sucking on the bone once again. She spoke. "They're all deceased." "My last husband died three years ago, that brown car that Jimmy is driving was his car." I damn nearly swallowed the bone. I got full right away behind that statement of four husbands dead and I made the 5th one; that was all I could think about. Not long after, I made my excuse to leave, and she was going shopping. I told her that I would meet her back at the house at 6:00 pm.

I did my daily routine of going to the office and talking to Howard. Today, I went over to the Black Marble to get a double shot of gin because I needed it. I spilled my guts out to Howard as he sat in the Black Marble, sipping on a beer in the booth across from me. I said, "Man, I make her 5th husband, I could understand it if I was the 2nd or 3rd one but the 5th. I told him, "Man, it's some bullshit going on here somewhere, Howard." "No wonder she has long paper." Howard replied, "What you mean, man, about her having long paper?" I told him, "Man, she had to have life insurance. A lady like that is working at the Public Aid Office owning three cabs, and having her own home that's already paid for. She had to have life insurance on all her husbands, or they had life insurance, and it was willed to her, either way, she got paid."

She would be a nice lady for me if I didn't have a wife and children waiting for me and if I could afford to eat out because I don't ever want to eat in her house again." "Then again, she could be death to me in more than one way." If she ever found out that I committed bigamy, she might be collecting off my black ass, or I could go to jail." "So, your ass is between the devil and the deep blue sea, huh, Al?" "No, Howard, I'm probably between the devil and death playing these little silly-ass games that I am playing with her." "I'm playing with my life and I'm too damn silly to understand this." You just can't fuck over women like I'm doing I'm getting ready to get out of this as soon as I can. This is a dangerous game I'm playing, and I took another swallow of my gin. Howard asked, "Get out of what, man?" "Are you talking about your marriage to her that you just got into?" I told him, "Get out of everything concerning Carrie." He asked, "How are you going to do that, man?" I said, "There's got to be a way, man, and if there's a way, I'm going find it."

It was about 7:30 pm when I reached 76th and Lafayette, I had stopped at the fish market and bought cooked fish for the both of us for dinner. Carrie was sitting watching television when I rang the bell. I asked her, "What about fish tonight, darling, would you like to have fish for dinner?" She asked, "Is that what is in the bag? She told me, "Well, I had fixed dinner. I cooked a roast, cabbage, mashed potatoes, and carrots, and I made my favorite corn muffins." I told her, "Darling, honestly, I just didn't want a full meal tonight." "Can you freeze it, and we'll eat it tomorrow?" "Can we do that, baby?" She looked at me and smiled and said, "OK, baby, let's go to the kitchen." She said, "What kind of fish do you have? I said, "Catfish, fries, and Cole slaw." She told me, "I don't want the fries, I just want the fish"

After I had gotten comfortable, we sat down to dinner. After making her laugh a couple of times and telling her how lovely she looked and how proud I was to be her husband, I sinned the lie to her. I said, "Darling, I can't go on riding what you at night in your cab, and my business is not taking on any new jobs for me to support you." : So, since we are married now and I have an obligation other than myself, I decided to take a job that Jimmy Roe has been asking me to take." "He is the foreman at the paint plant on 115th Street." "Since I am a contractor, he is going to teach me how to mix the paint professionally." Since you work at night driving the cab, I'm going to take the night shift from 10:00 pm to 7:00 am." "They pay pretty good money, and I can afford to look after you, honey." "On this little money that I am making now, I can't do that." "The car notes that you are carrying; I can carry." "So, this job will be helpful in more ways than one." She said, "I guess I can see that, but you don't have to strain yourself for me, darling." "I can't see you are working the night shift and then trying to run your business in the daytime." "That's too much, darling, don't you think?"

"Well, for a while, we can do that." "I can work the job for a while and then let it go because I will never let my business go." "So, you can brace yourself because I'm supposed to start tomorrow."

That night, I made passionate love to Carrie. That morning, after breakfast, I put the icing on the cake. I told her, "Carie, where did you say that spare key was that you wanted me to have?" "I want to move my things in today." She said, "I was wondering when you were going to move your things in here." "The spare key is on the chest of drawers in a soap-like dish, that's ok, baby, I'll go and get it for you." She went and got the keys and brought them back to me and explained what the three keys on the ring were for. She said, "This key is for the back gate and the front gate. "This key is for the garage, and this long silver key is for the front door."

CHAPTER 19

That next month I stayed closer to Nella, coming home at about 90:00 at night and leaving at about 9:00 the next day to go to the office. I had to try to give her and the kids some quality time with me to make up for those fishing trips that I had told her I had been going on. Then again, maybe I was trying to drown out the guilty feeling that I had about marrying Carrie. I don't know, but all my life I would mess up, and then I would get scared and try to fix it whatever it was, but guilty feelings are a bit stronger than other feelings. You must let them wear off. That's what I was trying to do, things for those feelings to wear off.

This street game was a bitch; you couldn't leave any loose ends. I had to tighten my hand up with Carrie by taking different sets of clothing by her house and hanging them up in her closet, and at the same time, I was telling my wife that I was taking them to the cleaners. Carrie was very happy to see all the clothing that I had brought to the house. It made her feel like I had moved home. Once a week I would come in and tighten my hand with her sexually. Everything was going smoothly. The hardest part every day for me was going by the house drinking a cup of coffee and leaving the cup on the table or dresser and making the bed look slept in so that it would appear as if I had been home.

For the last month, I have been working hard in my contracting business. Semi-big jobs and small jobs were coming through. I had met a white real estate owner who had given me a couple of jobs. Today, he sent me to a fire job at 1462 West Randolph. Half of the 2nd floor seemed to be burned up, and a portion of the staircase at the top landing. I gave him a price of $19,00.00 to repair it, the roof and all. He kind of asked me jokingly, "Maybe you would like to buy that building, Al?" "It would be something food for you since you're a contractor, and you can do the work on it yourself." I told him, "You might be joking, but how much do you want for it?" He said, "Oh no, I'm not joking!" "I can't give you a price right now." "But when you come in on Monday, I'll have the price for you." I said, "Good," and left.

I had a couple of drinks with Howard, Bullwhip, and Sug at my bar in the back of my contracting office. I told them about the offer I had gotten to buy the building. Sug said, "Al, do you have to come up with $19,000.00 to repair the fire damage?" "How are you going to do that?" I told her, "Fear not, Sug, an old man long ago showed me how to do magic and with Calvin, my carpenter, I can do it instantly" "With Calvin as my carpenter, Harvey as my painter, and Mr. Howard here as my chief laborer, it'll be a piece of cake." We all laughed, and before long, we said our goodbyes. I dropped Sug off at her home on 67th and Woodlawn, and then I went home to Nella.

It was a perfect day; the air was cool, and the wind was blowing leaves across the street. Paper flew in the air. It was just the right weather for my new outfit and my new leather coat with the cowhide. After I was dressed in black trousers, a black sports shirt, and that black Stetson hat that looked like a cowboy hat, I left to get the first Fizz. I felt like Superman that morning because I was sure that Mr. Nick Crosby, the real estate winner, would give me a price that I could meet. I felt like I was climbing upward in life. I headed for the little lounge called Michelle's on 63rd and King Drive which sat on the south side of the alley across from the Greyhound Bus Station. I had two drinks at Michelle's. The bar was empty; and I asked the bartender, Mr. Henry, "Damn, man, where is everybody?"

He said, "I imagine, well, some of the people said that they were going down to Marie's, the garden bar that sits there at 56th & King Drive." I said, "I've never been there." He said, "Yeah, man, it's pretty nice down there," "They have a combo band playing there, and that's what everybody is going there to listen to." "If you go down there, they have a big rod iron gate that sits right at the front sidewalk and then you walk into the garden." "You go throw another door into the lounge." "To make it easier on you, since you've never been the, just go through the door on 65th Street." "It's that big yellow building right there on the corner."

Before long, I parked my car on 65th Street about two to three car lengths from the door. When I got out of the car, I could hear the band playing. I entered the building, and there was a large stage where the combo band was playing. People were scattered around the room, talking, popping their fingers, and drinking. I walked up to the bar right at the door opening. A nice-looking stout woman who looked right at me came down and put a coaster in front of me. She asked, "Are you going to have a beer, darling, or are you going to have a drink?" "Welcome to Marie's, darling, and I am Marie." "I've never seen you here before." I said, "No, this is my first time coming here." She said, "OK." "We have a band here every Wednesday, Saturday, and Sunday if you care to come back. "Now, what are you having?"

I told her, "Give me a double shot of Old Fitzgerald." She said, "OK, and she was off to get my drink." She was back with my drink, and as I was sipping off the Old Fitzgerald, the whiskey was soothing to my throat. I was standing at the end of the bar, so therefore to the right of me was the garden. The door was open, and from the way I was standing, I could see a portion of the beautiful grass and flowers within the garden. My eyes left the garden to the open door and then beyond the open door at the first table I saw her, but when our eyes net, she quickly shifted her eyes to another direction. Just for the moment there, I knew that she had some interest in me. I took a sip of my drink again. I could see her staring at me again and then as quickly as he looked, she would turn her head away. She was sitting there with her back to the huge glass window. I imagine that was her girlfriend sitting next to her. Her back was also to the windows.

Two guys sat in front of them drinking, they had their backs to me. I could see her. No one at that table noticed me except her. I gave her the once over again while she wasn't looking. She was caramel colored with black hair. A part in the middle of her hair went back to meet the French Roll that she had her hair up in. Both sides of her hair were slicked back very tightly to the French Roll. She had on a beige dress that had a belt attached to it. She had the belt tied up into a bow in the back. Her shoes were beige pumps with straps on them that were tied up to her ankles. She stood. I could hear her tell her girlfriend, "I'm going to the bathroom."

She looked back at me again, but this time, she didn't turn her eyes right away; she looked for a moment, and then her eyes looked on the floor. As she walked toward me, I could observe her shape better. She was about 5'6" tall, had a small waist, medium hips, and nice legs that gave her that Coca-Cola bottle look. My eyes glanced back at the table she had left. The people at the table didn't notice her leaving. They were always conversing and socializing.

I looked at Marie behind the bar. She was stooping, putting fifths of whiskey on shelves. I stepped back into the lobby with my drink in hand. I was standing in front of the telephone booth when she tried to pass me. I kind of blocked her by stepping in front of her. I said, "Pardon me, young lady, would you know anyone who would be interested in a job as a secretary?" She looked at my shoes and her eyes slowly came up from my shoes as though she was undressing me with every look until your eyes set. That's when I noticed that her eyes were a beautiful gray color. She said, "Does it look like I need a job, sir, excuse me?" And she went into the bathroom. I stood there stunned and yet amused by her answer. This is a smart young lady I thought to myself. Very smooth, but I keep coming here she will give me that conversation I want I promised myself as I left out of the side door with my glass in my hand.

CHAPTER 20

Everything went smoothly for me for the next few weeks. Mr. Nick Crossby, the real estate owner, had given me a good deal on the building for $7,500.00 in total price. Our agreement was for me to pay rent in the amount of $200.00 per month until the $7,500.00 was paid in full. The rent was to start three months after the completion of the work, which was good because he gave me time to find some renters.

I had Calvin and two guys banging away on some 2X4s and 2X6s, putting a portion of the roof back together. I asked them, "Say fellows, how would you like to have a cold beer?" They said, "That would be fine!" I told them, "OK, I'll be back in a few minutes!"

At that part of Randolph, it was a one-way street going north about 1/2 block away from Ashland Avenue and a liquor store on that corner. I drove there, got the beer, and was leaving for the car when I bumped into Otha. He was a cousin to a houseman that I knew at Ann Hughes's place named Chuck. A sheriff's police officer was accompanying him into the store. "Al Wynn, he said as I passed him. Reaching for my car door, I looked up at him, and at first, I didn't recognize him until he spoke to me again. "Al, don't you remember me, Otha, Chuck's cousin, Ann Hughes's place?"

I replied to him, "Oh, yeah, how are you doing?" He said, "I'm doing fine, man, this is Robert." He introduced the sheriff's deputy to me. Robert, the sheriff's deputy, then spoke," Hi, man, how are you doing." I said, "Good." Otha was a short fellow who reminded me of Drug Store Johnny but not as big. Robert was about 6' tall, he wore glasses, and he had an open part on the side of his head.

Otha said, "Man, you could do us a favor if you're going south." "Robert came over here to get me, I work right there in this lounge, and I'm a bartender." "When Robert got off from work at the Bridewell Correction Center, he was coming to pick me up from work and give me a ride home." He had an accident in his car and broke an axle." "The car is next door at the mechanic shop." "They won't have it fixed until tomorrow." "We were going back to the lounge to call someone or call a taxi to take us home." "We can pay you if you're going back south." I said, "You don't need to pay me, you know that, but I need to drop this beer off to my men." "I just bought a building down the street." They said, "That's no problem at all."

I drove around the block to the building when I arrived there, Calvin and the guys were closing the hole up with plywood. I was very pleased at this because it would keep rain or snow from getting inside of the building. Calvin was a very good worker. I was thinking I should have bought them a twelve pack instead of a six-pack. They were pleased with the beer, and I left.

On my way home, Otha was sitting in the seat of the car. He was talking excessively about me. "Man, I tell you, Robert, this nigger, Al, they used to call him "Little Pimp." Then Robert would turn his head sideways and ask Otha, "Why did they call him "Little Pimp?" "Man, he was getting that money when he was young from those girls, bug talking about shooting dice." "Man, he could really shoot some dice to be a young man." "He really had it down pat." Robert said, "Yeah!" He said, "Yeah, man!" The conversation went on and on about shooting dice until we reached Michelle's Lounge on 63rd & King Drive.

They insisted on buying me a drink. The place was semi-crowded. Some people were dancing ti the music, some were on the pinball machine, and some were just sitting around at the table, and the bar drinking We were laughing and talking it seemed to me that Robert and I were bonding as friends I liked him, he seemed to be a nice fellow and intelligent. He wasn't like that; Robert was a slow talker. We started talking about the lounges, and Marie's Lounge came up in the conversation. "And what I like about Marie's Lounge," Robert was saying, "Is you don't have all the ghetto stuff like you have down here." Intelligent people come here, and they have a nice combo band also." "Most of the same people that go to the "Toast of the Town,' like Little Walter, Sunny Land Slim, Muddy Waters, and the rest of their crowd come to Marie's; and if they're not there, they go to the Toast of the Town." "Where is the Toast of the Town?" "Simultaneously, they said, "71" & Stony Island." I said, "That's right down the street from me." "I'm at 69th & Stony Island." "I never noticed the place." "The place is owned by Phil Rogers; you don't know Phil." I said, "Yeah, that's where he's at now." "He used to be on 55th Street."

We were laughing and talking about Phil when another guy came up to Otha and said, "Hey, Otha, where are you at now, I don't see you around 63rd Street anymore?" Otha turned to him and said, "No, man, I'm working up north in a lounge they call Barnes Blues Club." "You can ask my man, Robert; they get down up here." "All kinds of pretty young ladies be up there where I'm at," Otha went on talking. "All the pretty girls from the west side be up there." "Where's this place?" James asked. "It's on Randolph and Ashland; it's the northwest side." James said, "Give everybody here what they're drinking and give me another Bud, beckoning to Mr. Henry, the bartender." James sat on the bar stool on the other side of Otha. Henry turned to James and said, "James, I want you to meet Al, and he fellow on the end, his name is Robert."

We turned to James and gave him our hellos. After Mr. Henry placed our drinks before us, Otha turned back to me and said, "Al, do you live on 69th Street, or what are you doing over there?" I said, "No, I have a contracting office over here." "Oh, well, didn't you say that you just bought that building over there by my job?" I told him, "Yes, I just bought that building, and I've got a couple of guys putting that roof back together." James said, "I do construction work, do you need any other help." I said, "What kind of work do you do in construction?" He said, "I'm a hell of a floor finisher." "I do plaster, and I can do patching and cement." "I'm not a cement finisher, but I can dress the sidewalk up pretty good."

I looked at James; he was another heavy-set guy with a small beer belly. He was dressed in work clothes, and he seemed to have a pleasant demeanor. I said, "Well, James, if you're interested in doing that plastering that you know, give me a call." I gave him a card with "Al Wynn" on it, and he promised to call me the next day. I turned back to Robert, who was kind of looking at the television above the front window in the corner facing us. I asked him, "When do you be in Marie's, man, I mean, do you have a special day that you be there?" "What day do you be there?" He told me, "I mostly work evenings, and I go by there sometimes in the mornings and have a beer with Marie or something, but most of all, I come in on Saturdays when those pretty girls are here." "Most of the pretty girls are there on Saturdays." I said, "Well, man, I'm fixing to get out of here." "I'll probably see you over there; I plan to go over there on Saturday." He said, "Yeh, man, come on, I'll show you a good time at Marie's," I said my goodbyes and left.

CHAPTER 21

I hired James, and he proved to be a good plasterer, floor man, and a good laborer. So, I kept him around with me and Howard. The days dragged out until Saturday finally came. I dressed in one of my favorite suits. It was silk material, and the color was money green with shadowing stripes. I wore dark green Stacy Adams shoes with a hat to match. The silk tie that I wore caught the eyes of everyone. It brightened up the whole outfit. When I got there, Robert was sitting middle ways at the bar. Two or three stools were empty around him as I seated myself. "How long have you been here?" I asked him. "Oh, I've been here about an hour," he said. I looked around the room, and the whole place was crowded. You couldn't see the people at the tables for people standing.

I was on my second drink when I turned to 'Robert to tell him something about Howard. I looked over Robert's shoulder and saw her staring at me again. She was sitting in the same place that she was in when I saw her the week before. This time, she was dressed in a black pantsuit with a soft maroon color that fit into a bow at the collar. She was wearing black pumps. Her hair was in a bun, and she had a maroon-colored bun wrapped around the bun that matched her blouse. My heart seemed to beat faster as I whispered to Robert.

"There she is, man, the girl is sitting by the door that I told you about the other night at Michelle's."

Robert turned to look at her, then back to me, and said, "Yes, man, I know her through conversation." "I had a couple of words with her once." "She's a high-class girl, a fashion designer by trade." "I think she doesn't know that her shit stinks." "That fellow with his back to us in a white suit is her boyfriend." "He's a top-flight waiter at the yacht club downtown, he makes plenty of big tips." "I've talked with him, too."

Robert took a sip from his drink; I was listening to every word that he said. After the drink came down from his mouth, he turned back to me and said, "Yeah, man, that's a bad b road there." "As I said, she's a fashion designer. She makes all of her clothes herself." "Al, have you ever heard of the Dress Horsemen?" "No, I haven't heard of the Dress Horsemen." "It's about four to ten people in a club who are known for the outstanding way that they dress." "They are very well known in newspapers and magazines for their dressing." "She is one of the Dress Horsemen." I asked Robert, "What about her boyfriend?" "No, he doesn't belong; he dresses nice, but he's not a member of the club." He took another sip from his drink, and I took a long swallow from my drink. He turned to me once more and said, "No offense, but like I said, she doesn't talk too much."

I looked and toasted my glass to him, and I said, "Wanna bet!" He said, "Man, yeah, how much are you talking about?" I said, "Twenty dollars!!" "Twenty dollars bet, man," and he laughed and finished his drink. I said, "You can laugh if you want to, Mr. Policeman." "It's time for me to go to work, let me borrow your ink pen." He reached into his coat pocket and got his pen out. Simultaneously, I reached into mine and pulled out one of my contracting cards, and I wrote on the back. Robert told me," They call her 'Gin' for short," so I started with, "Give me a call, Gin, at your earliest opportunity," signed Al. I stopped the floor barmaid, and I kind of pulled her up close to me, and asked her, "Do you want to make $5.00?" She smiled and asked, "Doing what?" I told her, "You see that young lady sitting over there." She said, "Oh, you meant, Gin?" I said, "Yes." "Look, give her this card, but don't let the guys see it." She said, "I understand." The next time I see you, I'll give you another $5.00."

Before long, I saw her whispering in Gin's ear. She was very smoothly passing her the card because I didn't see it, and I was surely looking. When she finished whispering in her ear, she walked away from the table slightly, looked at me, and smiled. I knew then that I had been hooked up, and all I had to do was wait for her call. I said, "Come on, man, I'll take you to Michelle's and buy a drink, and from there, I'm going to call it a night." He said, "I'm with you, man, let's go." "I'll follow you in my car."

CHAPTER 22

Almost a week had passed; it was a Thursday, and I sat in my office behind the desk. Carrie sat across from me with her famous riding pants and knee boots on. The boots and pants revealed her shape. She had big legs and a nicely shaped body. Since I told her that I was off this Thursday, he wanted me to ride with her in the cab. She promised to buy me dinner. Howard and the rest of the people had left, and she sat here patiently smiling at me while I was talking to Calvin on the phone. I was saying, "Well, that's very good, Calvin. You'll be finished with that first floor soon, and I'll be able to rent it out." "Is that what you're saying?" OK, then, if that's what you're saying, then whatever material you need, just go ahead and tell Min Lu and have him add it to my bill." "Get whatever it takes for you to finish that job!!" I turned back to Carrie and smiled. I said, "I'm about ready, baby, are you?" She said, "Yeah, but instead of going out to dinner, I'd rather have some fish." "What about you?" I told her, "I'm with you, baby, whatever you want." "Do you want the fresh fish from Stony Island?" She said, "Yeah, we'll get it there." I began to rise from my seat when the telephone rang again. I shrugged my shoulders and smiled at Carrie again, sat back down, and answered the phone.

I said, "Hello, Al Wynn's Contracting." The voice on the other end of the telephone said, "You told me to call you." I recognized the voice on the other end as being Gin with that heavenly soft voice that she possessed. I was almost shocked that she had called so quickly, with Carrie staring at me, I was at a loss for words. I said, "Yeah, you know I was asking you if you want a job." "You know my girl, Sug, she has an uncle who died in Oklahoma." "She's thinking about moving out here, and I'm going to need someone in the office." Her answer came sharp and to the point. "I think I told you when I first met you, Mr. Wynn, I'm not looking for a job. And good night!"

I hung up the phone. The way she cut me off so sharply, I was embarrassed in front of Carrie. She noticed and asked me, "What's wrong?" "Well, Howard's auntie was interested in working, and now her husband told her that she couldn't take a job." Well, that's her thing." "Let's go out and get something to eat." As I had said before, I liked Robert being around me, especially over here on Stony Island when he had on his uniform and the big pistol hanging on his side.

It was Tuesday, and sometimes Robert would stop by like he did today and ride with me when I was doing my contracting work. After work, we would stop and get lunch or breakfast before he went home and went to bed for the evening shift. On this day, I was on my way to my building at 1462 W. Randolph. Calvin had finished the job, and I wanted Robert to see the finished work, and most of all, I wanted to tell him about the sway Gin had played me. After I told him what had taken place with the phone call. I told him, "Man, I couldn't say what I wanted to say, you know, with Carrie sitting there staring at me like she was doing." He laughed loudly and said, "Man, I know how you felt." You wanted to talk to this girl so bad and she called you man, and you couldn't talk to her." "That's a damn shame!"

After we finished looking at the building, I said what I wanted to say to Calvin and the rest of the men. We left for Gladys Restaurant on 45th and Indiana. Glady's was a famous restaurant that was known for its tender, flaky biscuits. Movie stars and comedians used to eat frequently at her restaurant. She was known from California to New York. Most of the restaurants were filled, and a lot of people were waiting for a table. So, we sat at the counter. After Robert and I had finished our meal, he turned to face me and asked me. "Hey Al, "How much are you charging for those apartments?" I said, "$375.00 a month for each apartment." He said, "They're pretty nice, man, I like them." "The thing is, I know a couple of guys who live on the west side, and they are looking for an apartment." "They would love that downtown action and right across from the park." I said, "Tell them to give me a call."

In the next couple of weeks, business was coming in strong. It had me running and jumping around Chicago. I missed seeing Robert for a couple of days. Sug was answering the phone and sending me off on leads to get contracts. Leads that would come from Skokie and north on Addison, all around Chicago, seven in the suburbs. My eyes were getting sharper now for deals on houses. Houses, I could almost steal. My little bankroll had grown from $4700.00 to $15,000.00. It was the following Friday that Robert came by to have breakfast with me at the Three Sisters Restaurant on 71st & Stony Island. Sug was going to be kind of late today. Robert sat behind her desk. The clock said a quarter until 10:00. I walked to the rear of the office to get a couple of beers out of the refrigerator when the telephone rang. I hollered back at Robert, "Get the phone, Robert!" As I opened the refrigerator door, I could hear him say, "Al Wynn's Contracting!"

Then, there was a muttering sound. When I came back into the office, he handed me a piece of paper with a lady's phone number on it. She wanted me to look at a garage. We both opened our beers and started to drink, then Robert busted out, "Oh, Al, I almost forgot out of breath from drinking the beer. "Man, I know what I wanted to tell you." I said, "What?" He said, "Man, I saw Gin Friday evening and told her what happened to you and how you had one of your little girlfriends there, and you couldn't talk to her, and she started to smile.' "I told her how you felt so bad about that happening." "Man, he's serious about you, and it hurt him the way you hung up and he didn't have a chance to explain. "The girl doesn't mean much to him, but out of respect for her, he wouldn't talk to you in front of her," I said, "what did she say behind that?" He said, "She was supposed to call you this morning." I said, "Man, you are bullshitting!" "Naw, man, I wouldn't play with you like that. I know how much you like that girl, and you're sincere, too."

I said, "Damn, Robert, I can dig where you are coming from, man, but don't you know that you're blowing that $20.00 we betted because if she calls, I'm going to cop her, and you're going to blow that $20.00." "If I thought it would help, I would give you five twenties for that girl because I know how much you want to cop her." I said, "Well, if I do, we're even." He smiled. We had finished the 3rd beer when Howard called and said he was on his way. Soon after Sug showed up for work, she spoke to Rober, put her purse on her desk, hung her coat by the bar, and proceeded to the bathroom. I asked Robert, "Damn, man, do you want another beer?" He said, "Yeah, just one more for the road, and I'm going home and going to bed, man."

Howard entered the door at that time, and I asked him if he wanted a beer, too. He responded, "Yeah, I need one." I went to get the beer. While I was taking the beer out of the refrigerator, Sug walked past me on the way to her desk. The telephone rang, and I could hear Robert answering, "Al Wynn's Contracting." When I entered the office, Robert was sitting behind my desk and talking on the telephone. Sug was seated at her desk, and Howard was sitting next to her. I handed Howard his beer and turned to Robert with his beer. He looked up at me and said, "Here he is and then handed me the phone and said, "It's Gin." He looked at me, smiling from ear to ear. I beckoned for him to get up and let me sit at my desk. I was seated, and I lifted the phone to my ear, and before I knew it, I was saying, "Hello, darling." She said, "Hi!" I told her, "This a complicated world, and I know some of the things I've been saying have made it more complicated for you." "I can untangle all these little webs if you'll have lunch with me tomorrow. The only thing you must do is tell me where and when."

She asked me, "Do you know where Walgreens drug store is on 47th and King Drive?" I said, "Yes." She said, "I'll be standing in front of that Walgreens at noon." I told her, "I'll be there," and I hung up the phone. Howard and Robert were staring at me when I stood up. Sug didn't seem to be concerned with what I was saying. She was looking in her bottom drawer for the pad that she used when she answered the phone. But the next word I spoke to Robert made her look at me, surprised. I said, "Robert, if you act like you want to put on a wig I would kiss you. He said, Man, don't you start, it must have gone well for you." I said, "Yeah, I have to meet her for lunch tomorrow."

CHAPTER 23

Finally, noon was here, and the big green Cadillac pulled to the curb in front of the door where she was standing. She was dressed in a sharp brown pinstriped suit with a waist-length brown jacket. Her hair hung loose, and the beige pumps she wore matched the beige turtleneck sweater she was wearing. I gave the horn a short beep. She didn't look at first. I had to pull up a little closer, right in front of her and I beeped again and leaned over toward the windshield so she could get a view of my face. She looked surprised when she was in the car. I asked her, "Did you eat lunch yet?" She said, "No." I asked her, "Where would you like to go to, Maybelle's or Gladys?" She said, "Maybelle's will be fine."

I drove the car onto King Drive and went south towards 51st Street. After parking in the lot we went inside and we went into the large dining room section past the eating counter. It was a nice dining room with mirrors all around. It was clean, cozy, and quiet. The waitress gave both of us menus and placed water before us. We were both reading the menu. The waitress stood there waiting for us to order. Gin told me, "Go ahead and order, I'm still looking." I was so used to pigging out and I forgot that I was with a lady. I told the waitress, "I'll have mothered liver." She said, "What would you want for the sides?" I told her, "I'll have the green and Lima beans, and I'll also have the beet and corn muffins." Gin kind of folded her menu and looked over at me.

The waitress asked her, "Are you ready?" She said, "Yeah, I'll just have a salad." The waitress asked Gin, "Is that all?" Gin replied, "Yeah." The waitress then asked her, "What kind of dressing?" Gin replied, "I'll have Blue Cheese Dressing, that will be fine." The waitress then asked us if we wanted anything to drink and I told her I'd have coffee and Gin told her she'd have grapefruit juice. I remarked to Gin, "No wonder you're shaped so nicely, you don't eat enough." When we were finished eating, she asked me, "What time is it because I want to be home by 5:00 pm." I told her, "That'll be fine." I didn't say another word. I turned the car around and headed for Hawthorn Racetrack, and halfway there, she said, "Where are you going?" I told her, "I'm going to the racetrack." I asked her, "Do you like the racetrack?" She answered, "I've never been to the race-tracks." I said, "Good, you'll have a thrill coming then."

When we entered the racetrack, I bought a scratch sheet for her and myself. We took a seat high up in the bleachers. The crowd of people excited her. I had a little time before the next race started. I taught her how to read the scratch sheet. I gave her a $100.00 bill to bet with. It was about the 5th race when she told me to get her 3,7, and 1. The trifecta of 3,7, and 1 came in and paid her $1,002.00. She was so happy, she just kissed me everywhere, on my face, nose, and ear, and she kept jumping up and down. She gave me the ticket, and I went to collect her money. After I brought her the money, she did not bet on the next race; she just kept counting the money over and repeatedly. When I came back from playing the 6th race, she gave me a roll of bills; it was $500.00. I told her, "I'm not like that, darling; that's your winning. She told me, "I wouldn't have had it in the first place if it wasn't for you, and I want you to have it." I took the money and put it into my pocket."

It was a joyful day until 4:00 pm when I had to take her home. I parked 1/2 block from her house. She explained to me that she had four kids and a husband. She didn't want me to think that she was a bad girl, but she and her husband just didn't click anymore. She had been thinking of leaving him for years, but for the kids' sake, she just stayed on. I kissed her lightly on her nose. She looked at me and said, "It's too bad that this day was so short." "I would have liked to take you out tonight for a drink or two. And I know this might seem selfish" …And before I could get out the words, she said, "My husband finishes at Penn Railroad at 3:000., and he's on his second job now and doesn't get off until 1:00." I told her, "Well, I'll pick you up at 7:00."

I went home to Nella and the kids and called over to my office, and told Sug to lock up and that I wouldn't be back today. I lay around the house and played with my children. Nella and I had fun playing with my little son, Jamie. He was so fat and cuddly. I have fun with my daughter, too. Of course, being a man, I had more fun with my son. I couldn't play with the girls like I could play with Jamie. Finally, I took a shower, got dressed, and headed back to 47th Street. I met Gin about ½ block from her house. She was standing there by the church, Greater Harvest, waiting for me. I knew where I wanted to take her. I wanted to take her to Toast of the Town, Phil's place. I longed to see Phil I pulled into the only parking space left in front of the building. The place was crowded at the front bar. Two stools were empty by the window. Phil was behind the bar with the barmaid. I looked up over the cash register, and there was a huge picture of Phil dressed cleanly in a convertible Eldorado. A white girl was sitting next to him. I looked at Gin, and then I scanned the room. When you first walk into the lounge to your left, two swinging doors resemble the doors in an old Western saloon. There was a round sign like a dish that hung over the doors and read, Chinese Food. On that same wall with the doors sat a couple of tables and two chairs. On the other side of the doors, you had three tables with two chairs at each table. To the right of the bar, there was another swinging door; you could hear singing and laughing. People were coming in and out of that door.

I finally caught Phil's eye and beckoned him over to me. I asked him, "What's going on, Phil?" He said, "My man, Al, Al Wynn!" "What's been going on, partner?" I told him, "I've been doing some light hustling." "I've got a place right down the street from you." He asked, "Doing hat?" I told him, "I've been doing contracting, of course." "Well, now, is that your wife?" I told him, "I wish it were." Phis said, "She's a beautiful young lady." We both said "Thanks" simultaneously. He asked, "What are you drinking?" I told him, "I'll have a Gin fizz." I asked Gin, "What do you want, baby?" She said, "I'll have a Margarita." Phil said, "The drinks are on me, Al." He asked me, "How long do you have now?" I told him, "A couple of hours." He told me, "Paula Greer and Gerri Mitchum are next door." "Do you want to go over and see them?" "They have a bar over there, too."

He told me, "If I'm not here when you get back, it was nice seeing you, Al." I told him, "You too, as we left for the other side. He went on to tell me, "They charge $10.00 to go in there on the other side, just tell Tim to let you in, you're my guests." That side of the lounge was very beautiful. The music was just coming to an end. As we entered the room, the lady said. "Let's give Buddy Young, on the piano, a big round of applause." The crowd applauded loudly. "Now, ladies and gentlemen," the lady said, I am Paula Greer, and let's welcome Gerry Mitchum to the bandstand." Gerri stepped on the stage, a very short lady about 5'6" tall with a small waist and big hips. She wore white shoes to match the long white gown with a bow on the side. She wore bangs, and her hair was shoulder-length. She grabbed the mike and hollered out, "Yeah!" "A ticket, a ticket, I lost my yellow basket," and the band joined in with her singing. Gin and I sat by ourselves, ordered our drinks, and enjoyed the music for the night. The clock on the wall showed 10:30. Gerri Mitchum was on the set singing, "Smoke Gets in Your Eyes." When we left the room.

I was back on 47th Street, now almost a ½ block from where Gin lived on 46th & Evans. I parked the car to let her out. She would be home one hour before her husband got home from work. She reached for the doorknob, and she turned slightly around to face me. "I had a lovely time," Mr. Wynn, she said. I told her, "So did I." If she wanted me to kiss her, I didn't make any move toward touching her or kissing her. "What time tomorrow will we have lunch or dinner, I asked her, looking very seriously. Without hesitation, she said, "Pick me up here at about 4:00."

I turned the car and headed for Cottage Grove, and I took a left turn on Cottage Grove to the outer drive. On the outer drive, I turned left and headed for home at 68th and Paxton.

The next day, I did my usual job. I met with Howard, and I talked with Sug, I asked Sug, "What could we do to improve the décor of the office?" she said, "I can't think of anything unless you want to get some blinds for the windows and the door because they would look more professional." I said, "Well, that's your next job." "Look in the Yellow Pages and find a company that sells Venetian Blinds, make sure that they will come out and take some measurements." I turned to Howard and said, "Come on, man, let's go and see how Calvin is doing the building on Randolph. "See you later, Sug." She said, "O.K."

Howard closed the door behind us. I had been keeping up a pretense with Carrie. Neglecting my family and spending most of my time with Gin. For some time now, Carrie had been bugging me about meeting my family. I told her that I only had one brother and a sister-in-law here in Chicago. For some time now, I had asked my brother to set up a day when he could invite me and Carrie to dinner. It was on a Sunday evening at his apartment on 51st & Drexel in Hyde Park, and I asked him again about the dinner. I explained to him about all the things that she had. That is when his wife, Jean, took over the conversation.

It seems like a good idea because I want to meet my sister-in-law." So, they set up dinner for that next Saturday. Jean was brown-skinned, with short hair with a part on the side. She was dressed neatly; she was twenty years old. She had little experience in life. My brother worked nights at the main post office. She always complained, saying she had nothing to do at night while he was at work. He would always listen to the complaints but would ignore them and go on doing what he was doing. We said our goodbyes until the following Saturday.

CHAPTER 24

I finally finished the building at 1462 W. Randolph and rented it out. The next week went by fast, with me partying with Gin every day, going to the racetrack, the bar, and then home. I would see Carrie between the hours of 4:00 when she got off and 6:00; then I would pick up Gin. My days and nights were pretty filled up with the jobs coming in I was making money and having fun spending it.

Saturday finally rolled around. We had finished dinner and were sitting in my brother's living room when Carrie spoke up, explaining how lonely she gets with me having a night job. Then Jean interrupted and said, "You and I are in the same boat because Daddy," referring to my brother, works nights at the post office." Carrie said, "Well, I am kind of lonely driving my cab at night. Maybe I can pick you up and you won't be so bored." She said, "That'll be so lovely." Carrie said, "Fine, we can start tomorrow night." I will pick you up at about 6:00 or 6:30." I didn't like that too much. I looked over at my brother. There was nothing I could say. I knew Jean ran off at the mouth and liked to get in other people's business, but I thought I could put a curve to that later. We sat for a while, said our goodbyes, and left.

It was about 2 1/2 months later I found out Gin that I had picked up one of my suits from the cleaners and stopped at my office to change. I brought Gin inside and seated her at my desk, and I went in the back to change. When I came back out, I asked her, "Would you like to go and eat, go down to the Toast of the Town? What do you want to do?" She asked me, "Can I ask you a question?" "When do you relax?" "Or should I ask, where do you relax when you relax?" I told her, "Believe me, I know where to go if you just say you want to go there." She said, "I'm with you." I told her, "Stay here for a minute, I'll be right back." I went to the corner of the liquor store. It was crowded with the usual people. I bought a pint of vodka and orange juice and some Kool cigarettes, and we were off to the Jackson Park Hotel right at 67th and Stony Island. Once inside the room, I mixed a short drink and drank it down, and she mixed herself a drink. I said, "I have one lesser shortstop to make, and I'll be right back." She said, "Don't be too long."

I got into the car and headed to 68th and Paxton. Once more, I went into my apartment. My wife was folded up on the couch looking at the television, and my kids were wrestling on the floor like they were cowboys and Indians or something. Once I was inside, they all simultaneously jumped up and screamed, "Daddy, Daddy!" They were all over me; my son was hugging my leg while I walked over to the couch and kissed my wife on the forehead. I reached into my pocket and gave my wife $500.oo to hold for me. I told a long, sad lie that I was gambling and not to wait up for me. She said, "Yes, man, with a look of disbelief and she put the money into her brazier and continued to watch television. I kissed my kids and went to my closet and got two joints out of my pocket.

Inside the car, I lit one of the joints. I wanted to be mellow and cool when I got back to Gin; I didn't want to be rushed. I wanted to play my hand the way it should be played. There was one thing I learned from Paula: it was never to rush a woman and to take your time. When I got there, I poured myself on another drink. Gin was sitting in a chair with her drink in hand. I placed the drink on the table by the bed and I undressed down to my underwear and folded my clothes neatly across the chair as Gin watched. I sat on the bed with my back to the headboard and looked over at Gin and told her, "Your clothes are lovely, darling, but they would look much better if they were folded on the chair.

Once having been a model, she acted the role for me. She removed her foot, and one slipper fell from her foot. She took off her stockings. She slowly undressed completely as I watched. She slid into bed beside me. I dimmed the light as I pulled her into my arms. I caressed her and kissed her body all over, making her anticipation grow stronger and stronger with every touch. I didn't make her beg as long as Paula did. I made love to her relentlessly. She stayed until morning. It was a beautiful night. It seemed after that night we bonded even closer.

One Saturday night, Gin had to get back early to her house because her husband was coming home early. She left me at the Toast of the Town and took a cab home. I was enjoying Gerri Thompson and Paula Sheets signing as I sat back and closed my eyes, listening to the keynotes of "Buddy Young," when a voice awakened me out of my imagination. "Did your girl leave early tonight?" she asked. I looked up into the sparkling eyes of Gerri Thompson. I said, "Yes, she had to leave!" She asked me, "Do you mind if I sit here?" I told her, "No, I don't mind." We sat there and had small talk. I bought her two drinks before it was her time to get back on the bandstand again. She said, "Is there any particular song you like?" I said, "Do you know, "Living For You?" She said, "Oh, Billie Holiday." I said, "Yes." She said, "Yes, I know it."

The MC said, "And now, ladies and gentlemen, Gerri Thompson!" She got to the bandstand and smiled a little cookie smile of hers. "Ladies and gentlemen, I'm dedicating this song to Mr. Al Wyn." I toasted my glass to her. She sang the whole song, and she sounded just like Billie Holiday. We ended up drinking the night away. I took her to breakfast at Mr. Biscuit on 69th and South Cottage Chicago. After breakfast, I took her home to 65th and Champlain. I arrived at my office at 8:45 am.

CHAPTER 25

Each night after Gerri dang "Living for You," she sang it and dedicated it to me every time I came with Gin. One night on a Wednesday, Gin made a crack to me. She said, "I know another admirer of yours, Mr. Wynn." I said, "Who's that?" "Ms. Gerri Thompson!" I said, "Oh, she's just being nice." Finally, Gin started inviting her over to the table to join us in a drink. We all became laughing partners, enjoying the afternoon together. Gin began accepting Gerri anyway she came.

It was a couple of weeks later that Gin had to go to her hometown in Florida. She would be gone for five days. Gin left on Thursday. I spent the nights listening to Geri, Paula, and Buddy Young. An hour before closing time, which was 4:30, she said, "Al, I want to ask you a question. "Do you smoke weekly?" I said, "Every day." "Well, I've got some real good week, but I can't smoke it at the house on account of my Auntie is there." "Can I grab some Chinese food from next door, and then we go to your house?" I said, "No, we can't go to my house. "I live in a building with eight men." I told her, "I can get a room if you like." She said, "Let's go."

Once we were in the room at the Jackson Park Hotel, I took the Vodka and orange juice that I had bought out of the bag. Gerri fixed the Chinese food, shrimp fried rice. We ate and listened to music on the radio. After we ate, Gerri asked me to go down the hall and get ice for the drinks. I did. It wasn't too long that I was back I the room with the ice. Gerri spoke to me from the bathroom, "I'm in here taking a shower, go on and make yourself a drink, I'll be out in a minute." I kicked off my shoes and was sitting on the bed by the nightstand with my drink resting on it. I was enjoying the music as I took a sip from my drink. Gerri walked out of the bathroom, unwrapping the towel that she had on her head. She looked like a young stallion. She was pleasingly tan with all her body parts intact. She had big legs that were bowed from the knee down. Her buttocks looked so firm that it seemed like you could sit on it. She took the refer from my bag and placed it on her nightstand along with a drink that she had fixed herself. She pulled back the sheet and got under it in the nude and said," Oh, that bath was so refreshing." I told her, "Maybe I should take one, too, if it was that good." She said, "Why don't you, I'll l roll some joints while you do."

I was in and out of the shower and lay on the bed and pulled back my side of the cover, and slid in beside her. She said, "Oh, I see that you enjoyed your shower, also." I said, "Yes, I did. She lit a joint and passed it to me. We had smoked about two joints each, and she said, "You know, I kind of like you, Mr. Wynn." She was whispering into my ear as I felt the soft, hot kisses touching my body. I lay there for a while, relaxed and enjoying every moment of it. Finally, I flipped the script and started making love to her. She kind of gave in to my touches. Not too long after that we were floating into ecstasy. She was asking me the next morning when I woke up and saw her brushing her teeth and fully dressed. She said, "It's 8:30!" What do you do in the mornings?" I told her, "My girl has the keys to my office, I guess she's there." I got up and brushed my teeth, cleaned up, and got dressed. I offered to take her to breakfast, but she said,

"No," so I drove her home. When I arrived at her house, she said, "I enjoyed myself very much last night!" I replied, "So, did I!" She mentioned, "I don't want our little friend to know our secrets." I said, "Right!" We said our goodbyes.

CHAPTER 26

Everything was going fine but it was less than two weeks when all hell broke loose. I was standing in front of mirror dressing in one of my finest suits with a tie to match, as I tried on my new gray Dobbs. I checked the tie and the neatness of the suit; it looked exactly like I wanted it to look. I had promised Gin that I would pick her up at 1:00 and we would go to the racetrack. I approached the lobby door, heading for the street. I almost went into shock when I looked through the glass door at the corner on the other side of the street where my car was parked, but now it was gone. I stood there on the sidewalk in front of the building, questioning myself. Did I make a mistake about where I parked the car last night or park around the corner?

There were few parking spaces on Paxton from 57th Street to 71st Street because of the many driveways the buildings had. I looked up and down the street on both sides. I did not see a money green car anywhere. I walked to the next corner, going east. I seemed to be getting dizzy from the feelings I had about the car. I rushed back to my apartment and called the police. A police car was sent to my house. After sitting in the back of their car, they questioned me and all. I was almost ready to get out of the car when they got a call from the station telling the police officers that my dealer had taken possession of the car.

I had given the desk sergeant all the information before they sent the squad car to me. The police officers gave me the name of the dealer and their telephone number and wished me a good day as I stepped out of their car. I rushed back to my apartment and called the dealer. The telephone rang, and the dealer answered the phone, "Hello, sir, can I help you?" he said. I said, "My name is Al Wynn." "I want to know what the shit you all are doing with my car." The dealer said, "Hold up, sir, you say our name is Al Wynn." "What kind of car do you have?"

I replied, "I have a Coupe Deville Cadillac." "Well, give me a minute to look the name up." It appears he was gone for an hour, but I guess fifteen minutes had passed before he came back to the phone and said, "Yes, sir, are you still there?" I said, "Yes, I am." He said, "Yes, sir, we do have the car, and you are not the owner." I told him, "My name is on the papers." He said, "Yes, your name is on the papers as the driver, but your wife, sir, is the co-signer, and she pays the car payment every month, and she paid us the down payment, and she is the only one who has a job." "If she says that she wants to take her name off the car, you cannot stand alone." "Now, if you want this car back, you bring us a co-signer just as good as your wife, and we might consider giving the car back to you."

I called Gin and she answered the phone. I told her that the trip to the racetrack was off because something came up. I told her that we would talk later. I called Carrie at work. She answered the phone on the second ring. I said, "Hey, baby." She said, "Hi, Al," in a dry kind of way. I asked her, "Why did you pull the car?" She replied, "Before I answer that question for you, Mr. Wynn, can you answer one for me?" I asked her, "What is it?" She asked me, "Why did you commit bigamy?" I told her, "What the shit are you talking about?"

She said, "If you don't know, I won't tell you, but I'll tell you this, I know about your wife, I know about your children, and I know the address to where you live and I do know if you give me any trouble about that car or anything else I will have a judge to resolve these problems for us."

I stood there with my mouth open as she hung the phone up in my ear. I remembered some years back, Odell had told me, "Once you cop a woman and lose her, you can cop her again if you go about, it in the right manner."

CHAPTER 27

It seemed like the whole world was closing in on me. The only thing in the world I thought I needed at this present time was a cold beer and a drink. I made my way to the Black Marble lounge two doors from my shop.

After thinking on my situation for about an hour, I thought I knew the answer to my problem. At about 11:00 that night I was drunk and could hardly stand. Howard and another guy helped me into a cab. I finally made it to my apartment where Nella undressed me;

The net day, I dressed very sharply. I was sober when I went to my office. I talked to Sug and Howard until 4:00pm. I had one beer that day. I knew what I had to do. I knew wht I had to say to Carrie. I had it all planned.

I arrived at 67th and Stony Island in a cab. The cab stand was two doors west of the Southmoore Hotel. I crossed the street from the Southmoore Hotel to the parking lot of the cab sand. I walked through the parking lot until I found Carie's car. I must have stood in that lot for fifteen minutes waiting for Carie to come out of the cab stand to her car. I noticed a tall slim guy walking towards me with his head down with both hands in his trench coat pockets. I stood erect and waited for him to pass me. He was almost to me when he raised his head to look at me that's when I recognized him.

I said, "Hello, Uncle George." It was my aunt Queenie's husband that I hadn't seen in years. He gave a grunt and kept walking. He walked to the end of the cab parking lot and turned and walked back to the other side across from me and then back to the cab stand. Standing here confused and wondering why he didn't speak to me. The way he was acting like he was a security for the parking lot. All this didn't seem right to me. The clouds began to cover the sun. The air seemed to become colder like it was going to rain. I felt a knot in my stomach. That nervous feeling that I had years ago had come back. It was always a sign of danger.

Something was warning me to leave that lot. As I turned to walkout of the lot, to the street I heard a man's voice call out, "Al, wait a minute." I turned to face him, it was Eddie. He said, "Come on pal, I'll take you home or would you prefer a drink." I said, "A drink would be nice." We were going down Stony Island to 69th Street. He said, "Man, you just had a close call, didn't you?" I said, "What do you mean?" He said, "Well, I was in the hotel when I came through the lobby into the cab stand and Eva tole me what was happening with Carrie and George Henry." He went on to say, "I heard George tell Carrie, I couldn't cut him, Carrie, that's my nephew." Carrie asked him, "What do you mean, your nephew; you never told me anything about a nephew, and how could he be your nephew and Eva's cousin at the same time, are you all kin?" Eddie told me, "I let them argue when I came out to get you." So, I asked him, "What's my uncle got to with Carrie?" He replied, "They were going together until she met you, Al, he drives one of her cabs."

We stopped at the Black Marble lounge near my office. Eddie and I sat for a long time drinking and discussing my uncle. I told Eddie some of the things that my father and my aunt told me about my uncle down in Georgia. He was greased lightening with that straight razor. He cut about five men down there and did two stretches on the chain gang. He was in jail when we came to Chicago.

Eddie said, "Well, you've got the Black Stone Rangers running around in the hotel, and Carrie is tight with most of them, including the twenty-one leaders in that gang." "So, if I were you, I wouldn't hang around this neighborhood any longer because you can't kill them all, and she really has it in for you." He went on to say, "You really hurt her pride, and you know what they say about a woman scorned."

After another hour or so of sitting there, I said my goodbyes to Eddie, and I walked him to his car. I walked toward my office as he drove away. I learned years ago, "Do not let your left hand know what our right hand is doing." I never let my friends or associates know where I lived. After Eddie drove away, I hailed a cab and went home.

CHAPTER 28

The next day when everyone was gone, I checked my bankroll, and I had $1900.00. Paxton was a long way from the main line, Stony Island, and the Livery cab stand. So, I did the long walk to 71st Street and hailed a Checker cab going west. I went right back to the old neighborhood where I used to buy my cars from on Western Avenue between 59th and 55th. I looked through those car lots. I found what I was looking for on 55th Street, a station wagon. After dealing with the sales agent, I got the station wagon for $1,295. Cash.

My next move was to find myself another store front. I searched for a place for three days. I was going north on Ashland when I saw a storefront for rent at 850t S. Ashland. The sign read:

GO ACROSS THE STREET TO THE REAL
ESTATE OFFICE

The real estate office was on the northwest corner of Ashland. I left my car in front of the storefront and walked across the street to the real estate office. When I entered the office, I told the receptionist that I was interested in the storefront across the street. She then directed me to one of the salespeople. He was short, bald, and talked really fast. Before I could get a word in, he led me over to the storefront, and he asked me as we walked. "What kind of business are you in?" I told him I was a contractor. He told me, "Good, I don't want it to conflict with the other businesses we have in the forefront."

It was a twelve-flat building with seven other businesses that extended from the alley and continued past 8505 S. Ashland. We were inside the storefront now and he told me there was a second part to that storefront. The building at 8503-8505 was a huge store-front where I could put my ladders in the back part of the store-front, the office was in front of it. There was a bathroom in the rear, in the corner. He led me through an archway to the other side of the room. There was a space about 10' by 10' that sat in front of a door in the rear. We walked into that room, and it seemed to be the main office with its private bathroom.

It had a desk in there and a couple of file cabinets, and I loved the setup. He asked me, "Well, young fellow, we have been renting this place for $250.00 a month." "If you rent the place and rent it now, you can rent it for $180.00 a month." "After two years, the rent will increase to $300.00, which I only fair." I told him, "That sounds like a good deal." "What do we do now?" He said, "If you want to pay your rent now, we can go over to the office, and I'll give you a receipt for your money and have your lease drawn up for the things we agreed on, then you can pick up the keys tomorrow."

I said, "That sounds like a winner." It had been almost a week since I talked with Gin. I gave her a call, and she seemed thrilled to hear from me. "Hi, Al, where are you and what happened to you?" I told her, "It's complicated, but I'll explain it to you this evening when I pick you up around 6:00." She said, "I'll be ready!"

After having dinner with Nella that night and enjoying my kids, I made it to Gin's at about 6:30. I told her everything. Later after I picked her up, I told her what my sister-in-law did to me. I told her about Carrie snatching the car from me. I also told her about buying the station wagon and how it would come in handy to help me with my business. I also told her about renting another office. I explained to her how it looked and the rooms it had. Before long, we were in front of the storefront. I showed her the two windows that went with the storefront. I said, "I'm not going ot lest you in because I don't have the key and I'm not going to let you in until I finish decorating it."

She said, "My, you've been through a lot of things this week, I don't see how you could have done all the things that you did. She went on to say, "these are some of the reasons that I like you, Al, you don't let anything get you down and you just keep on pushing." We headed for the Zanzibar Motel on 92nd and Stony Island.

CHAPTER 29

The next day, I went back to 8505 S. Ashland to the real estate office and got my key and picked up my lease. The next few days I was busy having the place decorated. I decided to choose 8503 to paint the whole place white. I decided for 8505 to paint it in Japanese colors, pink and red, with a red carpet and red curtains.

I concentrated on my contracting business after getting the place all decorated. I had to bring some revenue into place, and I started with my ads:

"NEED JOBS"

Carpentry, painting, concretem roofing

"CHEAP, CHEAP PRISES"

The next thing I had to do was hire a secretary and I put a sign in the window that read:

"HELP WANTED"

Receptionist to answer the phones and type three or four girls came to apply. I hired a 24-year-old college graduate. She understood the business. She knew how to type. I supplied the office with a typewriter for her to use. She also accepted the amount of money that I started her with. She started the following week.

I had to call on my mother for a loan. I borrowed $150.00 from her and headed straight to the crap house. I had to make enough money to pay my new employee and my rent. My luck wasn't as good as I thought it would be. When I paid my mother back $150.00, I had $450.00 left. I couldn't stop. So, the next day I was back again. My luck was a little better. I walked out of her with $900.00. The next few days I rested and went to enjoy myself on 47th Street. I thought about moving from Paxton.

CHAPTER 30

was downhearted about all the things that had just occurred in my life. I could see from my office window the taxi cabs rolling up and down the street. The night people go in or on their way out. It was about 11:30 am when God came to rescue me again. The phone rang! The caller asked, "Hello, is this r. Wynn, the contractor?" I said, "Yes, it is." He said, "Mr. Wynn, I have a house at 5138 Emerald Avenue hat needs half of a roof and window work, would you go and give me an estimate?"

I told him, "Sure, I can, but I'm pretty busy today!" I asked him if it would be all right with him if I went the next day. He told me, "That would be much better for me, Mr. Wynn." I asked him, "Would you give me a call tomorrow after twelve, about 1:00pm?" He said, "Fine." Then we hung up. Not too long thereafter, I was turning the corner onto Emerald looking for the address. There was a parking place right in front. I was very observant of the area surrounding the building. I noticed that the grass hadn't been cut for three or four months, there was a for-sale sign almost lying in the grass where someone had knocked it over. The front door was cracked open, whereas a person could walk right in, and so did I.

I was confronted with a huge living room. As I walked forward into the apartment, it had three bedrooms, a bath, and a full kitchen. I could see the stains that were in the hallway leading to the kitchen. There were the same stains on the kitchen ceiling tiles. As I walked into the pantry, I could see water stains in the corner and in some parts of the ceiling. There was a huge sun porch with screens around the windows. Some of the windowpanes were broken. I began to go up the steps to the second floor. I pretty much knew where the water started from and where it ended on the first floor. I was just getting ready to open the door when someone pushed open the door.

I said, "Oh, I'm sorry, I thought the place was empty." He said, "Not yet, but I'm trying to get the hell out of here, and Kate is, too." I asked him, "Who is Kate?" He said, "The lady in the front apartment." So, I started to ask him questions about his leak, and he said, "He didn't have any, and neither did Kate." While talking to Mr. Henry, I learned a lot about the building. I learned from Henry that an elderly woman had the building, but she died. Her nephew was coming over, keeping it up for her. After she died, no one was coming to keep the building up. I believed that she owed money to the real estate according to the lady next door. He told me, "And Kate would stay if they fixed up the building." That's when I butted in and told him "It seem as though someone is going to fix it up, someone called me form the real estate asked me to go and look at the roof and the windows." After that, it wasn't too long before I was saying goodbye to Henry. My mind was clicking like a time clock. I began mixing thoughts. Some of them were about Calvin, and all the things that Calvin had told me were coming back in bushel baskets to my mind.

CHAPTER 31

The next day, I called Mr. Henderson, he had given me his name and telephone number before he hung up the previous day. The phone rang for some time before he answered, "Henderson here." I said, "Mr. Henderson, this is Al Wynn." He said, "Oh, yes, the contractor, what do you have for me, Mr. Wynn?" I said, "First of all Mr. Henderson, I would like to ask you a question." "What would that be, Mr. Wynn?" He asked. I asked him, "Are you in the market to rent or sell that property?" "Well, I think that he wants to sell it. Why did you ask? Are you interested in it?" I told him, "Yes, I am." I told him "Maybe I could cut you a deal if I knew how much you want for the place." He told me, "Well, young man, I can find out, give me until about 5:00 or 6:00 pm and I can give you a ring back."

So, I messed around on 47th Street until about 2:30. Then I went home. I had a talk with my wife and played with my kids for the rest of the day while waiting for that telephone call. It was about 6:30 before he called and said, "Well, Mr. Wynn, I hate to tell you, but he wants $35,000.00 for it."

I figured out the needs of the house as follows: $4,000.00 for the roof and fix all leaks, plasterer holes throughout the building, and fix all the windows. Fix and replace all doors that need fixing and replacing throughout the house, and to replace or fix all banisters, steps, flooring, or whatever is need for the porches. The full breakdown in pricing for the completed job would be:

Full price	$13,000.00
Down Payment	2,000.00
Balance Due	11,000.00

The balance due will be the down payment on the house including painting on the inside and outside of the house. He said, "Well, Mr. Wynn, I'll give him the message and see what he says and I'll get back to you in a couple of days."

CHAPTER 32

That evening I talked with my wife about what he said. It was a two flat with four apartments in it. One in the rear and one in the front. So, we could rent out three apartments in the building and stay in one of the front apartments, which have three bedrooms with one bath and a kitchen.

The next couple of days I hung around the apartment waiting for his call. My wife and I both had anxieties about the place. The first thing she asked me the next day was: "Did he call you?" I told her, "This is only the first day." She said, "I know, I was just wondering." I told her, I was wondering, too." She asked me, "Oh, Al, I forgot to ask you, what about the back yard, is it big or small?" I told her, "I want to know too, so today, I'll drive by and take a look at it." After driving by and looking at it, I told her, "The yard is big and enclosed with a fence, there's a gate in front and the rear, a cyclone gate." I told her, "The people who lived there before left a two seated swing for the kids, the swings are made of iron and seem to be in good shape." "As I said, there are fences on both sides." It was hard getting through the next day.

I thought about what Eddie said, "Move and do it now." I needed that place. Even if I had to alter my deal by going back on the deal or offering a cheaper price. I kept looking at the clock. The clock read 5:30. It was almost 6:45 when the phone rang. Mr. Henderson was calling and said, "Hello, Henderson speaking. I said, "Oh, Mr. Henderson, I thought that you had forgotten about me." He said, "Oh, no, I didn't forget, but you know it's hard catching up with these young guys." "Well, Mr. Wynn, the young man, Carl, has accepted your proposal "We need to get together the first thing tomorrow morning or whenever you're available and close the deal." I thanked him and hung up the phone." My wife's eyes were bucked, looking at me. I said, "'We have it and everybody, even the kids, said, "Yeah!!!"

CHAPTER 33

It was 11:45 when I reached the address at 9211 S. Greenwood, the location of Mr. Henderson's home. I rang the bell, he let me in and led me to a big, huge dining room table. I, in return, reached into my briefcase and brought the contracts. I took one and gave him one and we both read them together.

He said, "Well, young man, it seems like these contracts are in order, I'll get a pen." I told him, "No, here's one right here." It wasn't too long before I was back in my car and thanking God. I made it to a payphone and called Nella. I told her of the good news. That evening, I thanked God for letting me meet Calvin. He taught me how to be more successful in life. My life continued to grow with the knowledge that Calvin had given me. All my life after that, when I did a job, I would thank God and Calvin. So far, it has been a wonderful life.